# Slashers

# Slashers

The Campaigns of the 28th Regiment of Foot During the Napoleonic Wars by a Serving Officer

Charles Cadell

*Slashers: the Campaigns of the 28th Regiment of Foot During the Napoleonic Wars by a Serving Officer*
by Charles Cadell

First published under the title
*A Narrative of the Campaigns of the Twenty-Eighth Regiment, Since Their Return From Egypt in 1802*

Leonaur is an imprint of Oakpast Ltd



ISBN: 978-1-84677-538-3 (hardcover)
ISBN: 978-1-84677-537-6 (softcover)

**http://www.leonaur.com**

Publisher's Notes

# Contents

To General the Honourable Sir Edward Paget, G.C.B.
Colonel, 28th Regiment, &c. &c. &c.

*Sir,*

Having had the honour of serving nearly thirty years in your gallant corps whenever they have fired a ball cartridge, during fourteen of which I commanded their grenadiers, I feel highly honoured by your granting me permission to dedicate a *Soldier's Narrative* of their services throughout the whole of that eventful and brilliant period, to one who has so often conducted them to victory.

I have the honour to be,
*Sir,*
Your most humble servant,
*Charles Cadell*
Lieutenant-Colonel, Unattached
Late Major, 28th Regiment

# Preface

I have but lately left the gallant corps in which I have spent the happiest days of my life; and being in possession of many anecdotes of officers and men, worthy of being known to their country, I have, with that view, employed my leisure in drawing up a brief account of their campaigns, of which I have been an eye-witness and participator for nearly thirty years. Imperfect as it must appear to many, by neglecting to give the features of the different countries and fields of battle in which we have been engaged, it must be understood, that from the rapidity of movements in the face of an enemy, it is impossible for the regimental officer to do more than glance at the surrounding objects. During an engagement, while doing his duty strictly and conscientiously, he has no time for general observations, or, consequently, for a comprehensive description of the scene of action; and when a partial cessation of the contest occurs, his mind is naturally occupied in the admiration of various feats of valour displayed, whether by friends or by foes. Thus, then, it will be seen, that mine is not a general history; and having aimed at nothing beyond a faithful record of facts connected with services in which the 28th Regiment took an honourable and distinguished part, I sincerely trust that my little work will be received by my brother soldiers in the same spirit with which it has been dictated.

## CHAPTER 1

# Expeditions to Germany, Copenhagen and Gottenburg

1802. On Christmas Day the 28th Regiment arrived in Portsmouth harbour, on their return from Egypt, and disembarked from the *Druid*, *Winchelsea* and *Blonde* frigates. Immediately on landing, they marched to Winchester, remaining there, however, only for a short time, and thence proceeded to Hilsea.

1803. In the spring of this year the regiment marched to Plymouth, where the second battalion was formed, by draughts from the army of reserve, drawn from the counties of Cornwall, Devon, and Somerset. On the 9th of July the officers of the different second battalions, then in progress of formation, appeared in that memorable *Gazette*, which gave greater promotion to the British army than has ever been known at any period of its history; and on the 12th of the following month, Colonel, now Sir Edward Paget, issued a brief code of standing orders for the 28th Regiment, preceded by an address to his corps, of which the following is a copy:

> In consequence of the great augmentation of the 28th Regiment, which is now to be composed of two battalions of 1,000 men each, by which a great number of young officers, as well as soldiers, must necessarily

be introduced into it, Colonel Paget has deemed it expedient to establish the following regulations for their guidance; and imperfect as they must be, yet he trusts that they may tend, in some measure, to promote amongst them a uniform system of discipline and regularity.

He earnestly desires every individual to recollect, that it is only by the most steady exertion, and by the most hearty unanimity and co-operation, that so large a body of men can be formed effectually, to take the field in a few weeks.

He most earnestly hopes to observe their rapid advance to perfection, proceeding from a spirit of emulation, and a laudable ambition to excel, rather than from any exertion of authority, or resort to rigid discipline, on his part. He feels desirous of impressing on the minds of all the young soldiers, that they have the good fortune of being incorporated with a regiment which, for upwards of a century, has been uninterruptedly employed in the acquirement of honour and reputation. He wishes them to know, that they have, upon their right and upon their left, comrades accustomed to victory, who have often met, and well know how to chastise, that insolent vain-boasting enemy, who, at the same time that he threatens our beloved country with slavery and desolation, knows, to his cost and to his shame, that in no one instance upon record has he dared to stand the attack of a British bayonet. He wishes every individual at once to consider himself an old soldier, and he will find that he is already more than half become so. He wishes everyone to listen with eagerness to those, who know from experience how to instruct; and it is not alone to the exertions of the officers and non-commissioned officers that he looks for assistance; but he fully relies upon the beneficial effects which will be produced by the general distribution of that stock of military information and instruction, which every old soldier has it in his power to dispose of to so much advantage.

Under the fortunate circumstance of being united to such a corps, Colonel Paget feels the most perfect confidence, that that proud spirit of superiority, which so naturally and so justly inspires the heart of every British soldier, will prompt each individual in his station to the most unlimited exertion of his powers, to render the 28th regiment at once an object of surprise and admiration to our beloved Sovereign and our country, of satisfaction and pride to ourselves, and of terror and dismay to the common and inveterate enemy of all mankind.

Plymouth Dock
August 12th, 1803

In the latter end of the year, the two battalions embarked for Ireland, and were quartered at Fermoy, forming there a brigade under the command of Brigadier-General Paget, who had recently been promoted to that rank, Lieutenant-Colonel Johnson being appointed to succeed him in the command of the first battalion.

1804. In the summer the two battalions were brigaded with the 28th, or Tipperary Militia. This corps, on account of bearing the same number, and from the similarity of their facings with the 28th Regiment, styled themselves our third battalion, which was afterwards the means of the regiment obtaining many volunteers from them.

These three battalions formed a brigade of the army encamped at Kilady, near Cork, under the command of Sir Eyre Coote; but at the close of the year they returned to their old quarters at Fermoy.

1805. In the spring of this year we marched to Birr, for the purpose of being brigaded under General (now Lord) Beresford, and in August encamped on the Curragh, as General Wilkinson's brigade of the army under Lord Cathcart; but on the breaking up of the encampment, the two battalions separated,—the first being ordered to Mallow, and the second to Dublin.

An expedition to the North of Germany having been resolved on by the government, the first battalion of the 28th Regiment, at the request of Lord Cathcart, was selected to form part of the army under his Lordship destined for that service; and after a very stormy and unfavourable passage,—in which two transports, one of which had the head-quarters of the 26th Cameronian Regiment on board, foundered at sea,—landed at Broomila, and marched to Bremen, where we remained six weeks in a state of inactivity.

1806. Re-embarking in the spring, the regiment landed at North Yarmouth from Cuxhaven, and in company with the first battalion, 4th Regiment, first battalion, 23rd Regiment, and first battalion, 95th Regiment, marched to Woodbridge, and afterwards moved to Colchester. In the middle of the year we changed quarters to Maldon and Danbury, remaining there until the 20th of July, 1807, when we returned to Colchester, and again prepared for active service.

## Expedition to Copenhagen

By the following order, the 28th Regiment was directed to embark again for foreign service:

Headquarters
Colchester
22nd July, 1807
The following corps are to be held in readiness for immediate embarkation:

| | |
|---|---|
| Major-General Spencer | 1st Battalion, 4th |
| | 1st Battalion, 23rd |
| | 1st Battalion, 79th |
| Brigadier-General Ward | 1st Battalion, 28th |
| | 1st Battalion, 92th |
| | 1st Battalion, 95th |

1807. On the 24th July, General Ward's brigade, which was afterwards composed of the 28th and 79th Regiments, marched from Colchester for Harwich, and, after having been inspected by Sir David Baird, immediately embarked on board the transports in waiting for us. In a few days we sailed, quite ignorant of our destination. After a very pleasant voyage, we arrived at the mouth of the Sound, on the evening of the 8th of August. The night was very dark; but a dreadful storm of thunder and lightning coming on, the vividness of the flashes fortunately enabled the whole of the immense fleet (we had been joined by the other divisions of the army from Portsmouth and the Downs) to anchor in perfect safety. The Danes were astonished to see such a fleet of men of war and so many transports casting anchor in their harbour, without the slightest accident, in the midst of such a storm. During the few days the fleet remained at Elsinore, we received much attention from the Danes; little did they suspect that we should prove such bitter foes.

On the 13th, however, some suspicions of our destination appeared to arise. The friendship of the Danes seemed to be cooling apace, and arms were distributed to the people in every direction. This was the last day we were allowed to land. Our intentions were evidently suspected; and on the morning of the 14th, at daybreak, we observed that a black Danish frigate had slipped off in the night from her moorings. The moment she was missed by the admiral, the *Comus*, sloop of war, was towed out by the boats of the fleet,—for it was then a perfect calm—and gave chase;—

this was a most beautiful sight The *Comus* overtook her in the Cattegat, on her way to Norway, and after a short action, captured her. This was the first act of hostility.

On the morning of the 15th, the fleet sailed from Elsinore, in the direction of Copenhagen, and at four o'clock, on the morning of the 16th of August, commenced landing at the small village of Wibeck, about eight miles from the town. This was the place where Charles XII. landed on his first campaign. We received no opposition; we only saw a few dragoons at a distance. The army advanced about four miles this evening, and that night we lay upon our arms in a barley field. This was the first night that many of us had lain out

On the morning of the 17th, our division, under Sir George Ludlow, consisting of the brigade of guards, and General Ward's brigade, moved on towards Friedericksburg, where there is a royal palace, close to a village of the same name. Here a curious circumstance happened. On our march we had reached the main road, leading from Copenhagen to Holstein. The brigade of guards were already upon it, and the music of the 28th Regiment; when a part of the royal family were seen, coining from Copenhagen, in their royal carriages. The moment they were known, the guards wheeled into line, opened ranks, and presented arms, the band playing "God save the King." What must have been their feelings to have been received in that way by a hostile army, on the way to besiege their capital! They were all females, and seemed much afflicted[1]. We proceeded to Friedericksburg, and bivouacked in the neighbourhood that night. Next day (the 18th) was employed in establishing ourselves. For some days our men were employed in

1. It appeared afterwards, that they were the two princesses, nieces to the King, who had solicited and obtained passports to quit the city. The King himself afterwards applied for the same permission, and passed through the hostile army in the same manner.

making fascines and gabions, and working at the mortar battery, which was destined to shower destruction on the unfortunate city.

On the morning of the 31st, while under arms, an hour before daylight, we heard a heavy fire of musketry on our left. We were all immediately on the alert, hoping that a part of the enemy might be coming our way; but in an hour's time the firing completely ceased. The enemy had made a sortie from their right, which was gallantly received by a piquet of the 50th Regiment, under Lieutenant Light Sir David Baird came up with the other regiments, when the Danes were repulsed with loss—Sir David Baird was twice slightly wounded, but did not quit the field. The attacking party of the Danes were the students of the University, formed into a corps of light infantry, and officered by their professors. They advanced in a most gallant manner, and fought nobly. Many of these young heroes were killed and many wounded. Such an instance of heroic devotion to their country, deserves to be recorded in letters of gold, and recalls the days of Rome and Sparta.

Two very extraordinary occurrences happened during the 31st. A number of those gallant young Danes had formed themselves into a corps of artillery, and were continually firing at the British from the ramparts of the town. A man of No. 7 company (Alum's), on a working party near the Ten Mortar Battery, was in the act of drinking out of his canteen, when a shot from one of their guns astonished him by knocking it out of his hands, without in the least hurting him. A party of the guards were likewise at work a little to our right, one of which was not so fortunate; he was standing with his cap off, when a shot from the enemy passed so near the crown of his head, that it killed him on the spot, without leaving the slightest perceptible mark. From several other instances of the excellent aim of these gallant fellows, we were all obliged to keep well under cover: the working parties were relieved in the dark, for nothing escaped these expert marksmen. The same afternoon, a fine milch cow, belonging to a native, was grazing near one of the batteries; the enemy supposing that she belonged to the besiegers, opened upon her, and very soon provided an excellent supper for our working party.

On the 1st of September, the mortar batteries being completed, General Peymaun, the governor, was again summoned, but without effect; therefore, about seven o'clock that evening, the mortars opened their tremendous fire upon the town, and with the assistance of the rockets, it was very soon set on fire. Nothing could exceed the awfulness of the scene: the hollow roar of the mortars, and the dreadful rush of the rockets—the shells of both sides passing each other in their revolving courses, dealing death and destruction wherever they fell. The bombardment continued until eight o'clock next morning (the 2nd), and at seven that evening the batteries again opened, dealing dreadful devastation on this unfortunate city, and did not cease until about eight o'clock next morning.

## To Copenhagen

On September the 3rd, in the evening, the batteries renewed their fire; again the town was in a blaze; the flames spread far and wide, and communicated to that beautiful building the Frei-kerke; in a short time its magnificent and lofty spire was enveloped in a sheet of fire, and in the space of an hour, fell in with a tremendous crash, which was heard for miles around; the light that issued from the ruins completely illuminated the surrounding country. The siege continued until the morning of the 7th, when orders were given for the formation of a flank battalion for the assault, composed of the grenadiers of the 28th Regiment, with those of the 7th, 23rd, and 79th, under the command of Major Browne. Their services, however, were not required; the town capitulated that forenoon at eleven o'clock, and the flank battalion immediately proceeded to take possession of the citadel and dockyard. In the course of a few days, when the necessary arrangements were made, and things became a little quiet, officers with passes, were allowed to go into Copenhagen. The sight was truly awful; 305 houses were burnt to the ground, and one church. The devastation and melancholy that reigned in that unfortunate city, it would require an abler pen than that of a soldier to describe. Parents were seen mourning for their children, and children for their parents. In several instances the murderous shells had forced their way into the very cellars, and destroyed mothers with their offspring at their breasts. Many were the brave hearts in the British army that deeply sympathized with the sufferers, and would have come forward to their assistance with that liberality for which they are so proverbial: but the Danes are a proud—a fine people, and bore their misfortunes without a murmur. Although our dangerous duties were now over, those of the working parties in the dockyard were far from easy, which service continued until the middle of October, when, by the extraordinary exertions of the navy, with the assistance of the army, the Danish fleet was made ready for sea. It would be but justice to mention, that the young men of the Danish Naval Academy vied with the students in the defence of their country; they assisted in manning the gun-boats and praams, and behaved throughout in the most gallant manner. They used to annoy the batteries on the right of the British line, by throwing sixty-eight pounds shot from their floating hulks.

On the 15th of October, we prepared to leave the beautiful island of Zealand, resembling the finest part of England. On the 16th the regiment embarked in the *Hercule*, seventy-four, the *Waldamaar*, eighty-four, (prize), and *Odin*, seventy-four, (prize), and on the morning of the 20th, the whole of the British fleet, each ship with one or two prizes, got under weigh from the roads of Copenhagen. What a sight it must have been for the unfortunate Danes, to witness the whole of their magnificent fleet borne away triumphantly. One, however, of the finest of our Danish prizes, the *Neptune*, getting aground, was obliged to be abandoned and destroyed, to prevent her falling into the hands of her late unfortunate masters. The transports that brought the troops over, were freighted back with the stores of their extensive arsenal.

In the afternoon, the whole fleet passed the Sound, with a leading wind, each ship with her prizes in her wake. The Danish flag was flying in the Castle of Cronburgh, and the batteries were all manned; but not a shot was fired. The fleet kept close to the Swedish shore, and what added more to the extraordinary sight, was the presence of the king of Sweden, who, having come down to Helsingborg to see the fleet pass, received a royal salute from every ship of the British fleet

After a most boisterous passage, we arrived at Portsmouth, and landed on the 2lst of November, and in a few days proceeded to our old quarters at Colchester. In this expedition we did not lose any men in our regiment, and had only a few wounded.

During the siege, that excellent officer, Colonel Smith, of the 82nd Regiment (afterwards Sir George), had a fortunate escape: he commanded at the Windmill Battery, on the left of the British line. One forenoon he was sitting in a chair close to the windmill, looking on the operations, when seeing something going wrong, he arose to give directions;—at that instant, a cannon shot from one of the Danish gun-boats broke the chair to pieces! During the time that the troops were employed in the dockyard, the British fleet in the roads had in the morning fired a salute, to commemorate some particular event, and in the afternoon, while many of the officers were at dinner, a report was heard as though a gun had been fired from the ramparts; soon afterwards another was heard, and then another: some of the officers thought it was another salute; but they were very soon undeceived by the splinter of a shell, falling on, and entering the roof of the house they occupied. It appeared, that a soldier of the 32nd Regiment, who had been placed sentry over some casks of fresh water in a shed, had taken up an old Danish firelock, which he snapped, not knowing it was loaded, it went off, and immediately a shell exploded, and set fire to some rubbish by which it had been concealed.

The shed took fire, and many explosions from shells followed in rather quick succession, both within the shed and outside, where they had been covered up with some straw. The fire in a little time became alarming, and the more so, it being in the immediate vicinity of a magazine, in which was stored a large quantity of powder; however, in consequence of the exertions of the 32nd Regiment, aided by the prompt assistance of those fine fellows the blue jackets, the fire was happily got under without the calamity of an explosion, which would have cost the lives of thousands. A melancholy accident happened on board one of the Danish vessels, which the 28th Regiment were assisting to fit out. A poor fellow, a carpenter, was working with his adze on deck, when a sailor, at work aloft, lost his hold, and happening to fell on the back of the carpenter, killed him on the spot, while he that fell escaped without a bruise.

1808. The regiment wintered at Colchester, and on the 19th of April 1808, the following order appeared:

Head Quarters
Colchester
19th April, 1808.
*Sir,*—In consequence of orders from his Royal Highness the Commander-in-Chief, I am directed by Lord Charles Fitzroy, to desire that the under mentioned corps may be held in readiness for immediate embarkation:

| | |
|---|---|
| 1st Battalion | 4th Regiment |
| 1st Battalion | 28th Regiment |
| 1st Battalion | 79th Regiment |
| 1st Battalion | 92nd Regiment |
| 3 Companies | 95th Regiment |

I have, &c.
(Signed) *J. Carey*
A. A. G.
Brigadier-General Clinton, &c. &c. &c.

On the 24th of April, this magnificent corps, consisting of five of the finest regiments in the army, received orders to march to, and embark at Harwich; the 28th and 4th forming the first brigade of the first division (under Major-General Frazer) of the army, under the command of Sir John Moore.

On the 4th of May, we sailed from Harwich, and arrived at Yarmouth on the 6th, when we received on board a number of additional officers to the staff.

On Tuesday morning, the 10th of May, the expedition sailed, and bidding *adieu* to the beautiful shores of Norfolk, steered with a fair wind to the northward. This naval part, under Rear-Admiral Keats, consisting of nine sail of the line, five frigates, sloops, and thirteen gun-brigs, with upwards of two hundred sail of transports. Our destination was strictly concealed.

On the 17th of May, after a pleasant voyage, we arrived off Gottenburg, and next day the *Mars*, seventy-four, and *Audacious*, seventy-four, piloted us into that excellent harbour. The head-quarter ship, the *Jenny*, was missing for four days, but arrived safely, after being nearly lost on that rugged coast.

The Swedes were quite astonished to see such a fleet. It was remarkably fine weather, and great numbers of the most respectable people from Gottenburg (five miles up the harbour from where we were lying) came down in boats, and rowed round the line-of-battle ships, which they much admired; and they were no less delighted with the bands of the different regiments that were playing on board the transports. The weather at this time was most delightful; there was no night.

The reports of our destination were various; but regimental officers were left only to conjecture. The first general order issued to the army gave universal satisfaction, and showed the judgement of the commander-in-chief, in selecting for such employment one, who afterwards justified, at Barrosa, the expectation even then formed of him.

The following is a copy of the order:

> Headquarters
> His Majesty's Ship *Mars*
> 20th May, 1808
> General Order
> Colonel Graham, 90th Regiment, has received his Majesty's permission to serve as a volunteer with the army, and is appointed *aid-de-camp* to the Commander of the Forces.

During the stay of the army at Gottenburg, we were amply supplied with provisions of every description. The men, for a piece of salt pork or beef, got as much of the finest fish as would serve them for four or five days; forty or fifty lobsters were generally obtained for a dollar. Every advantage was taken of the fine weather; the troops were practised to landing in the flat boats; and many other aquatic evolutions were found out for us, to the great amusement of the soldiers, and greatly to the credit of those who arranged them.

Divisions, brigades, regiments, nay, every officer of the staff, had his distinguishing flag. If our gallant commander-in-chief wished to see a division or brigade (there being nothing on shore but rocks), the signal was hoisted on board the *Mars*, the troops were on board the flats in ten minutes, and in five more in review order, in whatever part of the harbour the compass signal pointed out, every transport having boats for the number she carried. The regiment suffered a very severe loss, by the departure of Lieutenant-Colonel Johnson, the commanding-officer, who was obliged to return to England, on account of ill health. The following regimental order was issued on the occasion:

> Gottenburg
> May 30th, 1808
> Battalion Order
> Lieutenant-Colonel Johnson, being on the point of returning to England, to embark for North America, cannot refrain from expressing his regret, that any circumstance should render it necessary for him to leave the 28th Regiment, and he requests the officers to accept his most sincere thanks for their exemplary and gentleman-like conduct in every situation, since he had the honour to command it
> The character of the 28th Regiment stands too high to admit of any general remarks; but Lieutenant-Colonel Johnson feels the greatest pleasure in reflect-

ing, that the unanimity which has ever prevailed in the battalion, continues to distinguish it to this moment

Lieutenant-Colonel Johnson feels it a duty incumbent on him, to notice the very soldier-like conduct of the non-commissioned officers and men in general, and to assure them, that a continuance of it, cannot fail to entitle them to the approbation of their officers.

On the return of Colonel Johnson to England, the command devolved on Major Browne.

About the middle of June, a melancholy accident happened to our senior captain, Brevet Major Duddingston. He was walking the quarter-deck of the transport, when he saw two boys of the regiment clinging to the mast-head, and in calling out with a loud voice for them to come down, he burst a blood-vessel inwardly. He was immediately sent home to England, and just arrived in time to take leave of his afflicted wife before he died.

The expedition remained at Gottenburg till the 26th of June, when we received orders to be in readiness to sail, on the arrival of the Commander of the Forces. Sir John Moore arrived from Stockholm on the 29th, in consequence of some misunderstanding with the King of Sweden, and on the 2nd of July, the whole sailed on their return to England.

About the middle of July, the expedition arrived safely in Yarmouth Roads. After having been six weeks in the dreary harbour of Gottenburg, with nothing but rocks to look at, how delightful did the fertile shores of Old England appear to us! After procuring a supply of water, and of other necessaries, we sailed for Spithead, and arrived on the 20th. Everything was now done to supply the transports with water and provisions, as we had received orders to proceed on service the moment that the fleet was ready.

On the 24th of July, a general order arrived from the Horse Guards, which, droll as it may appear, gave universal delight; it was to cut off the men's *queues.*

A signal was immediately made for all hair-cutters to repair to head-quarters.

As soon as they had finished on board the head-quarter ship, the adjutant, Lieutenant Russell, proceeded with them and a pattern man, to the other troop ships. The tails were kept till all were docked, when by a signal, the whole were hove overboard, with three cheers.

CHAPTER 2

# The First Campaign in the Peninsula

On Sunday morning, the 31st of July, the expedition sailed from St. Helen's, with a fine breeze from the eastward; and on the 19th of August, after a delightful passage across the Bay of Biscay, we made the coast of Portugal. Next day, the army landed at Figueiras, on the Mondego, when Sir John Moore, receiving intelligence that Sir Arthur Wellesley had engaged and beaten the French at Roleia, instantly ordered the whole force to re-embark, whence we proceeded to Peniche. From the rapidity of the river Mondego, the landing and re-embarkation of the troops, was very dangerous; but from the excellent arrangements of the navy, no accident occurred. On the 21st, as we were sailing along the coast, we could plainly hear and see the firing at the battle of Vimiera. The sensation it created through the whole fleet was beyond description; what would we have given to have had a share in that glorious day! On the 24th, the fleet cast anchor in the Bay of Peniche, where we landed, and after a march of three leagues, joined Sir Arthur and his gallant conquerors on their field of victory. This was the most severe day's march we had ever experienced, for very few of us knew what real campaigning was till that moment:—the officers had landed with a change of raiment rolled in their cloaks, which was slung across the shoulders, besides carrying three days' provisions in their haversacks, on an August day in Portugal.

The men suffered much, having been on board ship since the 28th of April, excepting now and then a run amongst the Swedish rocks.

Sir Harry Burrard, having now taken command of the army, on the 27th Major-General Frazer's division (of which the 28th formed part) were ordered to advance from the field of Vimiera. The officers were now greatly relieved, as one car for their light baggage was allowed per regiment

The army advanced by easy marches, and on the 30th encamped at Torres Vedras, whence we continued to advance upon Lisbon. On September the 1st, Sir John Moore obtained the command of the first division, consisting of the following corps:

First brigade—first battalion, 4th; first ditto, 28th; first ditto, 42nd. Second brigade, first battalion, 9th; second ditto, 43rd; second ditto, 52nd; and five companies of the 60th rifles. Sir John Hope was removed to the second division, and occupied the height of Benefico, on the banks of the Tagus. During the time we remained here, we had the mortification to see the Russian fleet sail down the Tagus, with their colours flying; we were not aware that a convention had taken place, but had fairly considered them as lawful prizes. On the 16th of September, the first and second divisions encamped on the plains of Queluz, six miles from Lisbon. By this time, almost all the French troops had been allowed to embark, by a kind act of the convention, with all their plunder. Every thing was now done to have the regiment completed as soon as possible for further service. On the 22nd, the following regimental order appeared:

As the regiment will be inspected in two or three

> days, by Lieutenant-General Sir John Moore, Major Browne takes the earliest opportunity of acquainting the captains thereof.

At 7 o'clock a. m., on Monday the 26th of September, the 28th Regiment, comprising 1100 bayonets, under the command of Major Browne, was reviewed by Lieutenant-General Sir John Moore, on the plains of Queluz, in front of the camp. After going through many movements, Sir John made the most minute inspection of every man present, and expressed his admiration of the whole, but particularly of the grenadier company, which was then composed of 120 of the finest men the United Kingdom could produce. He returned to the right, and called Captain (now Sir Frederick) Stovin, and his officers, Lieutenants Kelly, Carroll, and myself, to the front, and thanked us in the handsomest manner for the admirable appearance of the men. He told us that they were the finest grenadier company he had ever seen—that they were a pattern to the British army, and he soon hoped to have occasion for their services. The compliment paid us, by such a man as Sir John Moore, was duly and highly appreciated.

On the 8th of October, 1808, the following general order was given out, which put us all in high spirits:

> Lieutenant-General Sir H. Burrard has received his Majesty's commands, to place a large portion of the army in Portugal, under the orders of Sir John Moore, to be employed on a particular service.

The 28th was one of the number. On the 9th we received orders to hold ourselves in readiness to march on the shortest notice. The baggage allowed was very little, each captain was allowed forage for one mule for company and self, and the subalterns a mule among them.

On the 14th and two following days, the first brigade, first division, consisting of the 4th, 28th, and 42nd Regiments, commenced their march for Spain by the following places: Santarem, Abrantes, Castello-Branco, and Guarda, where we were cantoned for a few days. On the 10th of November, we left Guarda, and arrived at Cuidad Rodrigo.

On the 10th, General Frazer, having again been appointed to the command of the division, gave out an order, part of which is as follows:

> He wished it to be explained to the men, that, on entering the frontiers of a people nobly fighting for their liberty, property, and very existence, with whom it was their good fortune to act against a most implacable enemy, to induce them to conduct themselves in the most orderly and exemplary manner; to accommodate themselves to the customs and manners of the inhabitants; and particularly to submit to such privations, as circumstances and the nature of the country through which they were to pass, might subject them.

Officers were recommended to wear the Spanish cockade in their hats, as a mark of respect for that nation; and red cloth ones were provided by the commissariat department for the men. The foregoing order had an excellent effect upon the men, and their conduct was exemplary.

On the 13th November we left Cuidad Rodrigo, and arrived at Salamanca on the 16th, when we found the following general order had just been given out by Sir J. Moore:

> Headquarters
> Salamanca
> 16th November 1808
> General Order
> The following order was written with a view to be circulated to the troops, on their entering Spain. By

some accident it was not received by the different generals to whom it was sent.

The Commander of the Forces, although from the reports he has received, he has every reason to be satisfied with the conduct of the troops, thinks it proper, however, still to be issued:

Headquarters
Lisbon
25th October, 1808
General Order

The Commander of the Forces trusts that the troops entering Spain, will feel with him, how much it is for their honour and advantage to maintain the high opinion, and cherish the good will, which that brave and high-spirited people entertain towards the British nation.

The troops on their march will generally be quartered upon the inhabitants.

The Spaniards are a brave and orderly people, extremely sober, and warm in their temper, and easily offended by any insult or disrespect which is offered to them.

They are grateful to the British, and will receive the troops with kindness and cordiality. This, the General hopes, will be met by equal kindness, on the part of the soldiers, and that they will endeavour to accommodate themselves to their manners, be orderly in their quarters, and not shock them with intemperance;—a people worthy of their attachment, and whose efforts they are come to support, in the most glorious of causes,—to free them from French bondage, and establish their national glory and independence.

Upon entering Spain, as a compliment to the

Spanish nation, the army will wear the red cockade, in addition to their own. Commanding officers will order them to be provided to non-commissioned officers and soldiers, and the expense will be paid by the Commissary General.
(Signed) *H. Clinton*
A.G.

## Retreat to Corunna

On the 28th of November, the 28th regiment was again put in the post of honour, as will appear by an extract from the general orders.

General Orders
The following changes will take place in the brigading of the army:—The 28th and 91st Regiments will form a brigade, to compose a part of the reserve of the army, under the command of Major-General the Hon. E. Paget.
Brigadier-General Disney will for the present assume the command of the brigade composed of the 28th and 91st Regiments.

By a general order of the 1st of December, the reserve was composed as follows:

| | |
|---|---|
| Brigadier-General Anstruther | 20th Regiment |
| | 1st Battalion, 52nd |
| Brigadier-General Disney | 1st battalion, 28th Regiment |
| | 1st battalion, 91st Regiment |
| | 1st battalion, 95th Regiment |

## To Corunna

At seven o'clock, on the morning of the 11th of December, the reserve, with Captain Carthew's brigade of artillery, left Salamanca, the other British divisions following in succession. Although the ground was covered with snow, we were all most anxious to advance, and leave our comfortable quarters, little thinking of the privations and hardships we were so soon doomed to undergo.

We arrived at Toro[1] on the 12th, where we were delighted to meet Lord Paget's brigade of Hussars, the 7th 15th, and the 18th, who had advanced from Astorga. Their appearance was magnificent, and they soon proved their superiority over the cavalry of the enemy. It was a singular occurrence, and truly honourable to the noble family of the Pagets—the meeting of the two brothers—each commanding the advanced guard of the two British armies. On the same day we arrived at Toro, Brigadier-General Stewart made a gallant attack on a party of French cavalry and infantry posted in the village of Rueda, with a part of the 18th Hussars. The enemy were completely surprised, the whole of them being either killed or taken prisoners. This was the first affair between the British and the French in Spain.

On the 16th, the reserve moved to Pueblo Douro, and on the 17th to Villapando. On the 19th, the reserve moved with the advanced guard of hussars. We reached Santarbas on the 20th, and Grajal del Campo on the 21st. Upon another gallant attack being made on a large force of the French cavalry, by Lord Paget, at Sahagun, in which they were cut to pieces, Sir John Moore gave out the following order:

Headquarters
Sahagun
General Order
The different attacks made by parties of cavalry upon

---

1. The band of the 7th Hussars played us into Toro, by order of Lieutenant-Colonel (now Lieutenant-General) Sir Hussey Vivian, that gallant officer having formerly served in the 28th regiment, while our Lieutenant-Colonel (Belson) had once been in the 7th Hussars.

those of the enemy, on the march, have given them an opportunity to display a spirit, and to assume a tone of superiority, which does them credit, and which the Commander of the Forces hopes will be supported upon more important occasions.

The attacks conducted by Brigadier-General Stewart, with the 18th Hussars, when upon the Douro, and that by Lieutenant-General Lord Paget upon the enemy's cavalry, at this place, are honourable to the British cavalry.

The Commander of the Forces begs that the lieutenant-general and brigadier-general will accept his thanks for their services, and that they will convey them to Brigadier-General Slade, and the officers, non-commissioned officers and men of the cavalry under their command, for their conduct in the different affairs that have taken place.

This handsome order made the infantry very envious of the cavalry; they longed to have an opportunity of meeting the enemy, and to follow the good example that had been shown them.

On the 23rd the reserve received an order to march in light order. At four o'clock in the afternoon, we moved off, in the direction of Saldanha, where Soult was posted; but the Commander of the Forces, having received certain information, that a strong reinforcement had arrived at Carrion from Palentia, found it necessary to stop the movement. The reserve retired to Grajal, and the army was ordered to halt until further orders. On the morning of the 24th, from the preparations that were making for a retreat, it was evident that the enemy was advancing with a superior force. The divisions of Lieutenant-Generals Hope and Frazer marched to Valdemora and Majorga.

On the 25th, just as Christmas had broke upon us, the

reserve, with the two flank brigades, commenced their retreats from Grajal del Campo, covered by the cavalry under Lord Paget, and followed the divisions of Hope and Frazer. The roads were dreadfully cut up by the guns, and there being a continual fall of snow, the ruts were entirely concealed, and the poor soldiers were continually falling into them. Captain (now Lieutenant-Colonel) Clifford, commanding the 58th Regiment, lost a boot in one of the ruts, and was obliged to walk the whole day without it. On this day Lord Paget fell in with a strong detachment of French cavalry; and with two squadrons of the 10th hussars, under Colonel Leigh, cut them to pieces.

On the 27th the reserve crossed the Esla, and covered the destruction of the bridge. We then retired to Benevente, where we were quartered in large convents. We rested two days, and were busily employed in repairing what we had suffered from the bad roads, and preparing for the retreat that was to follow, having had 150 soles and heels issued to each regiment.

We were now beginning to feel the rigours of winter, and but for the very judicious arrangements of our excellent commander, our sufferings would have been very great. Every officer and soldier had a new blanket issued out to him, and each regiment 150 pairs of shoes. On the morning of the 28th, the divisions of Hope and Frazer moved towards Astorga. The sick, and spare ammunition followed.

At daybreak, on the morning of the 29th, the reserve, with Colonel Crawford's brigade, left Benevente, leaving Lord Paget with the cavalry. About two hours after we had marched, a force of five or six hundred Imperial Guards crossed the Esla near Benevente. They were attacked by the cavalry picquets and 10th Hussars, under Brigadier-General Stewart, and completely routed,—leaving upwards of fifty killed and wounded, and seventy prisoners, among the latter of whom was General Lefevre, their commandant. We had the pleasure of seeing him pass the reserve, about two hours after the action. He had a sabre cut on his left cheek.

The reserve halted at La Baneza, during the night of the 29th, and at daybreak the next morning moved with the flank brigade to Astorga, where we arrived that afternoon, and found the Marquis de la Romana, with the miserable remains of his army.

What was our surprise to see such troops, instead of the fine army we had so often heard was to join us, 20,000 strong! and which, instead of being of any assistance to us, impeded the retreat of the British army, and exhausted the few resources that were left in this unfortunate country. Every house that we entered to shelter us from the inclemency of the weather was filled by those miserable beings, quite destitute of clothing and food.

The following is an extract of an order from Sir John Moore:

> Headquarters
> Astorga
> 30th December, 1808
>
> The present is a moment when the army is necessarily called upon to make great efforts, and to submit to privations, the bearing cheerfully of which is a quality not less estimable than valour.
>
> The goodwill of the inhabitants will be particularly useful to the army, and can only be obtained by good conduct on the part of the troops.
>
> The Commander of the Forces cannot impress too strongly upon the whole army the necessity of this; and he trusts that the generals and commanding officers will adopt such measures, both on the march and in cantonments, as will ensure it.

> It is very probable that the army will shortly have to meet the enemy, and the Commander of the Forces has no doubt but they will eagerly imitate the worthy example of the cavalry on several recent occasions, particularly in the affair of yesterday, in which Brigadier-General Stewart, with an inferior force, charged and overthrew the best corps of cavalry in the French service.

This order, giving such praise to the cavalry, made the infantry still more anxious. We longed to meet the enemy, who were not far off. The main body of the British moved on to Villa Franca. Sir John Moore and General Paget, with the reserve, followed.

On the 31st we marched to Camberas; the cavalry followed at night. The picquet, left to watch the advance of Napoleon and Soult, retired as they advanced.

1809. On the arrival of the cavalry at Camberas, about midnight, the reserve immediately moved on, and arrived next morning, 1st January, 1809, at Bembibre, just as the other division was marching off to Villa Franca. The scene of drunkenness that here presented itself was truly shameful. The stragglers from the preceding division, so crowded every house, that there was hardly a place to be had for the wearied reserve. Crowds of half-naked and unfortunate peasants of Romana's army, added to the confusion. On the 2nd, when Sir John Moore left Bembibre with the reserve and the cavalry, for Villa Franca, Colonel Ross was left with that excellent regiment, the 20th, and a detachment of hussars, to cover the town, while officers were employed in endeavouring to collect the stragglers. A few were got away, but many were so tired and lame from sore feet, that they did not care if the French sabres and bayonets were at their breasts, so completely did most of them give themselves up to despair. The rear-guard was at length forced to retire, and leave those unfortunate people to their fate. Some of those poor fellows, who had thought better of it, and were endeavouring to overtake their countrymen, were unmercifully sabred by the French cavalry, many of them in a defenceless state.

One of the handsomest men in the grenadier company, of the name of M'Gee, was coming along the road, lame from an accident, his firelock and pack having been taken by his messmates, to enable him to keep up; he was, however, overtaken by two French dragoons, and although unarmed and helpless, was inhumanly cut to pieces almost within our sight;—the exasperation of the grenadier company was terrible; they longed to have an opportunity to revenge the death of their comrade. The French were at last repulsed by the reserve at Cacabellos, about three miles from Villa Franca, where we remained all night, and took the duty of the rear-guard from the cavalry, who retired to Villa Franca, leaving a strong picquet in our front.

The village of Cacabellos is situated on a small rivulet with vineyards, and a commanding height in the rear. The river is passed by a bridge in the centre of the village, the banks being rugged but assailable.

January 3rd. The following occurrence had more effect in establishing the good conduct of the reserve than anything that had yet been done. We were formed in close column, on the Bembibre side of the river, when our gallant chief, General Paget, in an excellent address, called the attention of the soldiers to the dreadful and disgraceful scene of yesterday, and the merciless conduct the enemy's cavalry had shown to many of the stragglers. He told the men that they had now become the rear-guard of the army; and upon their sober, steady, and good conduct, the safety of the whole depended. Just as the general had finished his admirable and soldier-like address, and after all the orders had been given, and the necessary examples that had been made, two men of the reserve were found in the very act of shamefully plundering a house in the village, and ill-treating the inhabitants. The report was made, and the reserve was instantly formed in square; the culprits were brought out—the general being determined that an example should be made. They were ordered to be hanged upon a tree close to the village. Everything being prepared, the awful sentence was about to be carried into execution; the unfortunate men were in the act of being lifted up to the fatal branch, when an officer of the hussars rode into the square, and reported that the enemy were at that moment advancing. The general said he did not care if the whole French cavalry were coming up; that he would hang those men, who had been guilty of so shameful an outrage. At that instant a few distant shots were heard, and a second officer arrived at full speed with another report The general then stopped the execution, and turning round to the reserve, said, "Soldiers! if you promise to behave well for the future, I will forgive those men—say yes, in an instant."

"Yes!" was said by everyone.

"Say it again," said the General.

"Yes, yes!" was again exclaimed by all.

"Say it a third time."

"Yes! Yes! Yes!" and a cheer followed. The men were forgiven; the square was reduced; and the 52nd Regiment, under Colonel Barclay, went through the village in double-quick time, and in the most beautiful manner took possession of the vineyards on the opposite side of the river; while the remainder of the reserve crossed the bridge under cover of the 95th, and formed on the hill behind the 52nd. By this time the enemy were close upon us, and attacked the 95th in great force, the cavalry joining in the onset. They were terribly galled by the Rifles, as they advanced through the village. The 95th then retired up the road to the right and left, the French being at the same time exposed to a murderous fire from the 52nd, in the vineyards, which completely checked them. The 52nd then retired up the road, when the enemy were again most gallantly repulsed.

The French in this affair lost the general officer commanding the advanced guard, and many men. A column of them was also severely handled by Captain Carthew's guns, and stopped descending the hill on the other side of the river. This kept them quiet until the afternoon of the 5th of January. Our gallant Commander-in-Chief was present during this affair, and where-ever there was a shot fired, was he always to be found. This was the first time the infantry had met the enemy. In the evening the reserve retired to Villa Franca, where we expected to obtain provisions; but to our great disappointment, everything had been plundered by the stragglers of the preceding divisions. Major Browne was the only person who succeeded in getting anything. He procured a piece of salt pork, which he tied to his holsters; but it was very soon cut away, for we were marching in the dark.

The enemy being very near, at ten o'clock at night we moved on, and made a night-march to Herrerias, where we arrived at midnight, and after a few hours' rest proceeded towards Nogales. We had not advanced far, when we fell in with a large convoy of wagons, with supplies for the Spaniards, crossing from one part of the country to the other, which looked very suspicious, just as the French were advancing. It was fortunate our haversacks were empty; and as it was impossible to take the wagons with us, the shoes, bad as they were, and the trousers, were hastily served out to those who wanted and would carry them. They were a most seasonable supply, as the very heavy falls of snow that had taken place rendered the roads in such a dreadful state, that our shoes were almost all worn out. Several officers and men were actually without.

On our way to Nogales, and passing over a mountain covered with snow, on the top of it we witnessed a dreadful scene. Two Spanish wagons had been upset, under which lay the bodies of two men, and a woman with a babe at her breast, all frozen to death. There had been some bags of bread in the wagon with them, as there were some crumbs and dust remaining. The men were in such a state from hunger, that they absolutely moved the bodies to collect the snow, and picked out the fragments of bread as they went along.

We reached Nogales in the afternoon, and found it full of the unfortunate stragglers from the Spanish army, with nobody to direct them. Of course, after these people and the divisions that preceded us, very little was left for the reserve.

I must not omit an excellent action of a soldier of our regiment,—Private Shea, of No. 8 company. He had been sent forward on the commissariat guard, and when every thing had been expended, he was left at Nogales to rejoin the regiment. He by accident discovered a quantity of very fine potatoes; and having procured a boiler, by the time he thought the regiment would arrive, had a large quantity ready boiled; and as we passed the house he was in, served them out two or three to each officer and man, nobly making no distinction, as he knew we all had suffered alike. This was indeed a most seasonable and unlooked-for relief. Our hands were completely benumbed, having marched over a mountain covered with snow, with a shower of sleet in our faces.

I was quartered with a number of my brother officers, in a house which also contained a Spanish general with two *aids-de-camp*. We were drenched when we came in, and in taking off our clothes before a large fire to dry, I placed a valuable watch on the chimney-piece, and going to the door to direct some stragglers where they were to lie down, found on my return that a Spanish *aid-de-camp* had taken the liberty to walk off with it. On awaking the noble *Don*, who was lying in an adjoining room, covered with warm skins, to report the circumstance, he replied in a surly manner, that "he could not account for the people he had about him.

On the morning of the 5th, the reserve left Nogales. We were detained at a bridge a little way on the road, covering the engineers, who were endeavouring to destroy it, but they did not succeed. The 28th Regiment was now the rear-guard of the reserve; and the flank companies, with a company of the 95th, formed the rear-guard of the regiment. The whole distance was a continued skirmish. About noon we came up with two cars laden with dollars; but the bullocks that drew them being completely exhausted, it was impossible to save the treasure. Under these circumstances, Sir John Moore decided that the whole should be thrown down the mountain, most judiciously considering, that if the casks were broken, the men would make a rush for the money, which would have caused great confusion, and might have cost the lives of many. The rear-guard, therefore, was halted; Lieutenant Bennet, of the light company, 28th Regiment, was placed over the money, with strict orders from Sir John Moore to shoot the first person who attempted to touch it It was then rolled over the precipice; the casks were soon broken by the rugged rocks, and the dollars falling out, rolled over the height—a sparkling cascade of silver. The French advanced guard coming up shortly after to the spot, were detained for a time picking up the few dollars that had been scattered on the road.

While we were still retiring in continued action with

the enemy's advance, we heard firing to our left, and in a short time saw a number of Spanish stragglers, filing down towards us, firing as if they were skirmishing; an officer was sent to know what was the matter, when they very coolly said, "they were firing to warm their hands!" The reserve reached Constantine, where some rum had been saved. As much as was advisable was served out to the troops, and as the enemy were advancing in great force, the remainder was destroyed.

Sir John Moore, thinking the enemy would annoy us in retiring down the hill at this place, halted the 95th, and artillery at the top. The French likewise halted their column for more than half an hour. As soon as the reserve had reached the bridge, the rifles and guns retired, and the whole passed in safety, without losing a man. The enemy in a short time came down the hill in great force. General Paget was then ordered to defend the bridge with the 28th and 95th Regiments, while Sir John Moore drew up the 20th, 52nd, and 91st Regiments in a strong position on a hill to the rear of the bridge. The 28th went to the right of the road, the 95th and artillery to the left. The position was hardly taken up, when the attack commenced. The enemy's *chasseurs à cheval* came down close to the bridge, and immediately commenced skirmishing, every eighth man holding the others' horses. They were supported by a very heavy column of cavalry, at which the artillery made beautiful practice with Shrapnel shells. The first shell burst over them, but getting a better range with the second, it fell right into the centre of the column, and not being accustomed to musket bullets sent amongst them in every direction, the enemy were put into the greatest confusion. After a few rounds, they were obliged to retire, having suffered severely. The 28th and 95th gave their skirmishers a smart peppering, and they were frequently repulsed in their attempts on the bridge.

The French were now in great force, but we retained our position. The skirmishing continued till dark. The enemy suffered a severe loss; but from the admirable manner in which our position was taken up by General Paget, our loss was very trifling.

At 11 o'clock at night, General Paget withdrew the 28th and 95th. On rejoining the other regiments, we retired towards Lugo, and arrived next morning, very much fatigued. We were quartered in the neighbourhood, and supplied with provisions.

The dreadfully disorganized state of the advanced divisions, drew from Sir John Moore a very severe order, and on the 6th it had its good effects. On the morning of the 7th, the French commenced a cannonade, but were soon silenced by our artillery; and in the evening an attack was made on the right, but repulsed by the 51st and 76th: both these regiments behaved most gallantly on this occasion.

The following general order was issued on the evening of the 7th.

> General Order
>
> The army must see that the moment is now come, when after the hardships and fatiguing marches they have undergone, they will have an opportunity of bringing the enemy to action.
>
> The Commander of the Forces has the most perfect confidence in their valour, and that it is only necessary to bring them to close action with the enemy, in order to defeat them; and if it be a complete defeat, as he trusts it will be, it will in a great measure end their labours.
>
> The general has no other caution to give them, than not to throw away their fire at the enemy's skirmishers, merely because they fire at them, but to reserve it until they can give it with effect.

On the morning of the 7th, the reserve advanced from Lugo, and took its place in the line; and on the 8th the army were all in position, ready and anxious for action. The commander-in-chief rode frequently along the ranks, and was quite pleased to see every one at his post. All day, the army remained anxiously waiting for the French to attack; but Soult, thinking he would have a better opportunity, remained quiet. About 10 o'clock that night, the different brigades began to retire by Lugo, leaving their fires lighted.

The movements of the army were so admirably arranged, that the enemy had no knowledge of our retreat, until daylight of the 9th. The reserve did not retire from Lugo until 10 in the morning. The rain fell in torrents the whole of the night and day. The following order was given out:

> It is evident that the enemy will not fight this army, notwithstanding the superiority of his numbers, but will endeavour to harass and tease it on its march.
> The Commander of the Forces requests that it may be carefully explained to the soldiers, that their safety depends solely on their keeping their divisions, and marching with their regiments; that those who stop in villages, or straggle on the march, will *inevitably* be cut off by the French cavalry, who have hitherto shown little mercy to the feeble and infirm, who have fallen into their hands.
> The army has now eleven leagues to march: the soldiers must make an exertion to complete them, the rear-guard cannot stop, and those that fall behind must take their fate.

Every attempt to preserve regularity on the march, was altogether ineffectual The corps which suffered the least from straggling were the artillery, the guards, and the reserve. Using Sir John Moore's own words—

The artillery consists of particularly well behaved men; the guards are the strongest body of men in the army, and consequently suffered less from fatigue, besides they are strictly disciplined, and their non-commissioned officers are excellent The reserve was commanded by an indefatigable officer, and the regiments that composed it were admirable.

The march from Lugo to Valunda was dreadful, the troops being exposed to a heavy rain the whole way, and when the different columns arrived, after resting as well as they could, they moved off again in the evening. The want of shoes, sore feet, and bad roads, knocked up many, and rendered it impossible for them to keep their ranks. From the masterly manner in which the British army was withdrawn from Lugo, it gave us several hours' start of the enemy, and it was not till the afternoon of the 9th, that our rear-guard began to feel them.

General Paget, with the reserve, was ordered to halt, and take up a position for the protection of the stragglers some miles from Betanzos. We were very badly off for provisions, and on that account a party under the command of an officer was sent out to the road, and took from every straggler a part of what he had. We very soon had a good store of flour, some potatoes, bread, bacon, &c.—enough to serve out a proportion to the whole of General Disney's brigade. On that afternoon, a considerable force of French cavalry came upon some of the stragglers. A sergeant of the 52nd, who happened to be behind looking after some of his men, collected a considerable number, and gallantly repulsed the cavalry, by which means he saved many that would otherwise have fallen into the enemy's hands. The reserve remained in this position, all drenched with rain; and on the morning of the 10th moved, and bivouacked on the heights above Betanzos.

Here we met with a Godsend for the night: just as we had taken up the ground, we found a number of wagons laden with dry bullocks' skins, on their way to Corunna; we made beds of some, and covering of others, which gave us for once a dry sleep. On the morning of the 11th, the other divisions having left Betanzos, the reserve abandoned their position, and moved through the town. The 28th took possession of the bridge on the other side, while the engineers prepared to blow it up: the other regiments were formed on the hill above, leading to Corunna. The enemy's cavalry came up, and endeavoured to interrupt the operation, but were gallantly repulsed by the 28th. A sergeant of the Imperial Guards, more daring than the rest, charged to the very centre of the bridge, when a gallant fellow, Thomas Savage, of the light company, stepped out to meet him, and taking a deliberate aim, shot him dead on the spot. Savage had just time enough to take possession of his cloak, when a party came up, though too late, to the assistance of the Frenchman. We were now under a heavy fire, the French having. occupied Betanzos in great force, so that we were obliged to retire without accomplishing our object, covered by a part of the 95th, posted on the hill. A slight skirmish between our rear and the enemy's advanced guards, amused us on our march to Corunna, where the other division of the army had already arrived. The guards and General Frazer's division were quartered in the town, and General Hope's occupied the suburbs. General Paget, with the reserve, after passing and destroying the bridge over the Mero at El Burgo, took possession of that and other villages on the St. Jago road. We had now finished our terrible retreat; but what was our disappointment when we found no transports to receive us! The French came up in the evening, and took up a position on the other side of the river, and were in their turn no doubt disappointed, when they found the British out of their reach, arrived at Corunna, and in comfortable quarters. Next morning, at daybreak, we saw that the enemy had mustered in great force. Our amusement for some time was for the British and French officers to fire at each other across the river; but as soon as General Paget found it out, he put a stop to it. Fortunately we were well covered, and there was no harm done.

On the 13th, the reserve was removed to a village near St Lucia, within a mile and a half of Corunna, to rest after their fatigues and hardships.

On the morning of the 14th, a little after daybreak, while sitting by our arms, in case of an attack, on a bridge on the road to El Burgo, some of us lying on the parapet, we were aroused by a terrible explosion: men and officers flew to their arms. In a few seconds another was heard. Some thought the enemy had opened a murderous cannonade, and were about to pour destruction amongst us. We soon, however, discovered to our great delight, that it proceeded from the explosion of 4,000 barrels of gunpowder, that had been sent from England for the use of the Spaniards, and was destroyed to prevent its falling into the hands of the enemy. Such an immense quantity was too much to explode together, it was therefore divided into two, and although three or four miles from Corunna, many of the windows were broken. Major Browne was the only person who knew what was to take place, being told by the commanding officer of artillery on his way to give directions; but he had no idea it was to be to that extent.

The French were in as great a panic as we were; their army was under arms, and *aids-de-camp* flying in all directions. In a short time everything was quiet; but a shower of white ashes begun to fall, and continued for some time afterwards.

We had now the comfort of fine weather to dry our

clothes; the men were enabled to make themselves tolerably comfortable, and on the afternoon of the 14th, what a welcome sight presented itself—the whole fleet of transports, convoyed by numerous ships of war, sailing round the citadel, with a fair wind. Our privations, our fatigues, everything we had suffered, were forgotten, in the idea of returning to our native land, and proud to be able to say, that we had heartily thrashed the French whenever they dared to come near us.

On the 15th of January, the enemy advanced to the spot where the magazine had been blown up on the day before; a little skirmishing took place to the right, but the reserve was quiet in its cantonments, enjoying a rest and preparing for embarkation.

On the forenoon of the 16th, all our sick and wounded were embarked, and we received orders to follow them at three p. m. At a little after two we began to fall in, when the cannonade commenced, and instead of going to our ships, we were marched off in double-quick time to the field of battle. General Paget received orders to advance with the reserve, and support Lord William Bentinck's brigade, the 4th, 42nd, and 50th Regiments. At this time—when the 42nd and 50th Regiments were severely pressed by superior numbers—Sir John Moore rode up, and in the most energetic manner said, "Forty-second, remember Egypt!" and seeing Majors Stanhope and Napier, of the 50th, behaving so gallantly, said, "Well done, my two majors!"

The former was killed, and the latter severely wounded. We moved up and formed close columns in the rear of those gallant fellows, the enemy's cannon shot ploughing the ground about us in every direction, and now and then plumping in amongst us: the battle was now raging in our front, and strong columns of the enemy were moving to their left.

General Paget, by a rapid and judicious movement, hastened to our right with the reserve. The Rifles and 52nd dashed on, and very soon repulsed the enemy. Another strong column of theirs was moving up the valley. General Paget attacked them with part of the reserve, and drove it back. The French, seeing their left threatened, withdrew their columns. The battle now raged on the left and centre; the enemy were driven back in every direction; night closed in; and victory was the reward of our exertions. It was about the middle of the fight that we heard of Sir John Moore being mortally wounded. It added fresh vigour to the troops;—they were determined to be revenged.

About ten at night we moved off to Corunna to embark. The transports having room for troops had lights at their maintops; but owing to the darkness of the night, the confusion was dreadful. The different corps were all mingled together; but it blew very hard, and we were glad to get on board the best way we could.

The masterly manner in which our lamented commander-in-chief brought off his little army, in the presence of an enemy superior in force, with every advantage from their resources in their rear,—after so harassing a march, fighting and beating them, when his cavalry and artillery had been embarked,—commanded the admiration of the whole military world, and therefore requires no comment here.

On the 17th it was intended that the different regiments should be removed to their own ships; but the enemy bringing some guns upon the heights of St. Lucia, which commanded the harbour, began to knock the dust out of the sides of the old transports, so that they were all obliged to cut their cables, and put to sea[2].

---

2. Our baggage animals were all left on the beach. Major Browne was fortunate enough to get a pig in exchange for a horse. The major was rather unlucky with his pork; for in the hurry of embarkation, piggy was taken on board one ship, and the major on board another.

We were thus in a dreadful state; not a soul could get on board the ship which contained his baggage and sea-stock. It was fortunate we had a fair wind. On the 26th of January we reached England; part of the regiment arriving at Portsmouth, and part at Plymouth. We remained a short time at Portsmouth to recover from our fatigues and hardships, and then marched to our old quarters at Colchester.

All our animals were left on the beach at Corunna. I recollect but one exception. The wife of Serjeant Monday, the orderly-room clerk, actually carried a lap-dog in a basket over her arm, throughout the whole of this dreadful retreat, and brought it home to England with her.

The loss of the 28th on this retreat was reckoned at between two and three hundred men. No returns of the killed, wounded, and missing were ever made out; it was found to be impossible. Two officers, Lieutenant West and Quartermaster Hill, died from the effects of their sufferings in the hospital at Plymouth. On the advance of the regiment into Spain with Sir John Moore, about 200 men of our regiment were left in hospital at Lisbon. They afterwards formed part of the first battalion of detachments[3]. The officers of the 28th Regiment left with them were Captain Bradbey, Lieutenants Briggs, Gilbert, Huddlestone, Irwin, and Eason. Their gallantry was most conspicuous at the memorable passage of the Douro, on the 12th of May, 1809, in the brigade under the command of Sir Edward Paget, who unfortunately lost his arm. The reduction of Oporto followed.

This little band of "Slashers"[4] was so fortunate as to be severely engaged at the glorious battle of Talavera, where

---

3. What might not that corps have done? It could boast of a company or detachment from ten of the best regiments in the service—the 20th, 28th, 38th, 42nd, 43rd, 52nd, 79th, 91st, 92nd, and 96th.

4. The 28th acquired this *nom-de-guerre* when they wore swords; I believe it was in the early part of the American war.

they gained immortal credit for their corps by their gallantry. Captain Bradbey and Lieutenant Gilbert were wounded; Lieutenant Irwin, though not hit, suffered a loss which was reckoned a serious one in those days; a doubloon, rolled up in the skirt-pocket of his coat, was unfortunately carried away by a musket shot.

In the autumn of 1809 this gallant detachment joined the second battalion on their arrival in the Peninsula.

## Chapter 3
# Expedition to Walcheren

1809. On the 28th of June the 28th Regiment left Colchester, to be again placed in the post of honour, forming, with the first and second battalions, 4th Regiment, Lord Dalhousie's brigade of the reserve, under Lieutenant-General Sir John Hope. The other brigade was composed of Highlanders, under Sir William Erskine. We arrived at Dover on the 4th of July, were inspected on the 11th by his Lordship, and on the 14th by Sir John. Both of them expressed to Colonel Belson their satisfaction at the fine appearance of the regiment.

On the 16th, at five in the morning, we left Dover for Deal, and embarked at nine—the right wing on board the *Lavinia*, Lord William Stewart, and the left on board the *Salsette*, Captain Bathurst. On the 28th, this, the most magnificent expedition that ever left the British shores, composed of 40,000 of the flower of the army, sailed from the Downs. It was one of the proudest sights England ever witnessed, there being upwards of 600 sail, and an immense musquito fleet of gunboats. The day was delightful; the chalky cliffs of Ramsgate were covered with people, and with, our glasses we could plainly see the waving of handkerchiefs from hundreds of fair hands. Many a fine fellow left his native shores that day, not doomed to fall in the field of honour, but by a dreadful pestilence!

On the morning of the 29th we descried the low land of Holland, and at eleven o'clock, a. m. came to anchor opposite the town of Campvere. The reserve was on board the squadron under the command of Sir Richard Keats. The 29th was employed in boiling and getting ready our three days' marching provision of salt pork and beef, and making preparations for landing.

The 30th still proved unfavourable; but it moderated in the afternoon, when Sir Richard, with Sir John Hope, shifted his flag to the *Salsette*, on account of it drawing less water than the line of battle ships. Soon after we arrived, a telegraph belonging to the enemy was seen working very rapidly on shore, close in our vicinity.

Sir Richard, after consulting a short time with Sir John, made a signal for the carpenters of the squadron with their tools, and in the meantime four companies of the 28th, under Major Browne, got into the boats. When the boats arrived from the other ships the signal was given, and the whole pushed off, the troops leading, and pulling for the shore.

The moment the boats touched, the water being very shallow, the "Slashers" jumped out, and very soon drove a picquet of the enemy from a strong position at the telegraph a considerable distance into the country—giving time for the carpenters to land, who quickly levelled the mast and house to the ground. The fall of the telegraph was received by three cheers from the squadron—the rigging and yards being completely covered with sailors and soldiers intently watching the little expedition. The service being accomplished, Major Browne retired with the troops, and immediately re-embarked, taking with him all the signals and books belonging to the station.

On the 1st of August the reserve landed on South Beveland. The weather was very fine, and the sight was beautiful, 150 boats being employed on the occasion. After the division was formed and inspected by Sir John Hope, Lord Dalhousie's brigade went into the following cantonments, the first battalion of the 4th to Graven-polder,—two companies to De Gresse, patrolling to Ebbersdyke,—the second of the 4th to Abskirh, patrolling to the sea,—the 28th occupying Clocting, and patrolling in front to Capelle and Bieslingen, facing the East Scheldt, which was now completely commanded by our squadron.

Fort Batze a strong fortification on the south extremity of the island, was taken by the guards under General Disney, from which we could plainly see the enemy's fleet, seven ships of the line, under the protection of Fort Lillo, close to Antwerp, on the left bank of the river.

South Beveland was very soon cleared of the enemy, their forts taken, and all made prisoners. On the 5th of August the 28th moved forward to the delightful villages of Capelle and Bieslingen. On the 7th, we moved to Biddersdyke, situated in a small bay, opposite to Bergen-op-zoom, where we completely overlooked the enemy. On the 7th, we were inspected by Lord Dalhousie on the alarm post. The French attacked Fort Batze, with gunboats on the 8th, and got a severe chastisement from our artillery and the gallant guards,—our loss was inconsiderable.

Our brave comrades in arms, the British tars, had now the command of all the passage round the Islands, with their numerous gunboats,—those of the enemy, whenever they appeared, were glad to seek shelter in Bergen-op-zoom.

On the 11th the French gunboats made another attempt at Fort Batze, but were beaten off with loss.

The gallant blue jackets, on the 13th attacked a number of their armed boats,—they sent one into the air, and seven to the bottom. The batteries being now finished before Flushing, about 2 pm. the bombardment commenced; the roar was dreadful, the fleet joining in the scene of destruction—the town was set on fire in every direction.

On the morning of the 14th a squadron of frigates, under the command of Lord William Stewart, forced the passage of the Scheldt under a heavy fire from Flushing and Cadsand; it was returned by the ships with great effect, they received very little damage, only one shot hitting the *Lavinia.* In the afternoon of the 14th the cannonade suddenly ceased, and silence succeeded the roaring of the bombardment; we all hoped the town had surrendered; but in about two hours we again heard the work of destruction commence with redoubled vigour, which continued until about two in the morning of the 15th, when they capitulated. During this severe service, the Royals, 5th and 35th Regiments, had opportunities of distinguishing themselves. Captain Hay of the light company of the Royals, and Captain Arthur of the 35th, were particularly mentioned in general orders.

The reserve now eagerly hoped to be employed against the enemy's fleet, lying almost within our grasp under the guns of Lillo; we however remained quiet in our cantonments, laying in large stores of the Walcheren Fever, and we envied our more fortunate comrades before Flushing, who had the consolation of a few hard knocks to accompany it; at the end of August, we left this grave-yard for Britons and returned to England, where we again occupied our old quarters at Colchester.

We had hardly settled, when the dreadful fever broke out amongst us.[1] It was truly melancholy to behold the numbers that were cut off: every evening about dusk a string of from eight to ten fine fellows were carried to their graves! The deaths were so numerous that a corporal and eight men only attended each funeral.[2]

---

1. I was the only officer of the regiment who did not smoke during the expedition to Walcheren, and the only one that escaped the fever.

2. On one of these melancholy occasions, a ridiculous occurrence took place; an Irish corporal and eight men of the (continued opposite)

Previous to leaving Colchester on the Walcheren expedition, Colonel Wynch commanding the 4th, Colonel Ross of the 20th, and Colonel Belson of the 28th, agreed to try grey trousers made in different ways. The 4th had them made tight, with black gaiters, the 20th, as overalls, with buttons down the sides, and the 28th loose, with half boots. On our return, they were compared; those of the 4th were all torn at the legs, the buttons were off the overalls of the 20th, while those of the 28th were nearly as good as when we started. The grey trousers, as first worn by the 28th Regiment, were thus adopted throughout the army, to the great comfort of the soldier.

---

grenadier company of the 28th went to bury a fine fellow who had died the day before,—the dead house at the hospital being full of men of different regiments, our corporal was taking away by mistake, the body of a man of the 43rd, when a non-commissioned officer of that corps claimed him: "Sure," says Paddy, "I am come to bury a man, and isn't it now all the same which regiment he belonged to? I am only just taking the best looking one."

## Chapter 4

# The Second Peninsula Campaign

1810. At the latter end of January, the second battalion of the 4th and 28th, embarked at Portsmouth for Gibraltar, in transports under convoy of the *Jamaica* frigate, Captain Lycet. We encountered a dreadful storm off Cadiz; two transports with the 4th went on shore near Fort St Mary's, and were all made prisoners; one, with a part of the 28th, passed the French batteries, and got safe into Cadiz without any damage: the remainder of the fleet succeeded in getting through the gut of Gibraltar, and landed the troops at The Rock.

Notwithstanding the change of climate the terrible fever still followed us; we lost many men, and a most valuable officer in Captain Hill, who was by his brother officers justly and sincerely regretted; a monument was erected to his memory at Gibraltar.

On the 13th of April, Major Browne left Gibraltar, with four light companies and a party of artillery under Lieutenant Mitchell, and took possession of the old Moorish fortress of Tariffa (celebrated afterwards for its gallant defence by Colonel Skerrett in January 1812, with the 47th and 87th regiments); on the 20th they were attacked by a strong force of the enemy, who were most gallantly beaten back, and pursued some distance by Major Browne and his brave garrison; one artilleryman was killed.

The enemy still having possession of an old convent and some houses that annoyed the flank wall, Captain Stovin of the 28th, and Lieutenant Shipley of the engineers, led a sortie of two companies of the 28th,—supported by Captain Mitcham and his Spaniards,—out by the water-port gate, and drove the French in the most gallant manner nearly as far as the pass of La Pena. In September, Colonel Belson being obliged to return to England in bad health, the remainder of the regiment embarked for Tariffa, to be placed under the command of Lieutenant-Colonel Browne. We were here frequently employed in repelling the marauding parties of the French from the lines before Cadiz, but particularly in the end of January, 1811.

1811. An attack was projected by the boats of our squadron, then before Cadiz, on the French lines. The Spanish General Bigenes, with a brigade, was to assault Medina Sidonia simultaneously with the squadron, while we were to advance from Tariffa with a corps of Spaniards trained under that excellent officer, Captain Mitcham of the 28th Regiment, to cover him and to threaten the French left. We advanced eighteen miles to the enemy's advanced posts at Casa Vieja; the weather was dreadful, and there were no houses in the neighbourhood to afford us the least shelter. Lieutenant Anderson volunteered to storm the church and some houses of which the French had possession; but from not having ladders, and our force being so small, it was thought injudicious. After two days' suffering from rain and cold, having, in addition to the inconvenience of the weather, a deep river to ford, when we moved from our nightly bivouac to the position we took up by day, an express arrived at Tariffa to say, that from the boisterous state of the weather, the attack from Cadiz could not take place, and with orders to Lieutenant-Colonel Browne to return.

No other officer being then at Tariffa that could be spared, Assistant-Surgeon Johnston volunteered to be the bearer of the despatch to Lieutenant-Colonel Browne. He had arrived within a short distance of our position, when unfortunately for the poor doctor—his uniform being concealed by a cloak—he was observed by some mounted Spanish guerillas, who took him for a French officer endeavouring to escape; he was instantly attacked, and before he could make himself known, they had broken one of his arms, and cut him dreadfully about the head and body, inflicting thirty-two wounds—though none mortal, As soon as he was dressed, four of us holding a blanket over him to keep off the rain, carried him to our bivouac for the night; and next morning we returned to Tariffa. Our advance was of great service, as we diverted a large force of the enemy towards us, which enabled the Spaniards to take Medina Sidonia. On our return to Tariffa, the following general order was received from Lieutenant-General Campbell, the governor of Gibraltar.

Gibraltar
4th February, 1811
General Order
In consequence of a despatch received from Brevet Lieutenant-Colonel Browne, 28th Regiment, commanding at Tariffa, relative to the movements of the troops under his command, directed to co-operate with those of the Spanish nation, under Brigadier-General Bigenes, in the attack of Medina Sidonia, which was carried.
It is with the greatest satisfaction that his Excellency the Lieutenant-Governor is afforded an opportunity of publicly thanking Lieutenant-Colonel Browne, for the able and judicious manner in which he conducted the service allotted to him on that occasion,

which reflects the highest credit on his military talents, and to which Brigadier-General Bigenes bears ample testimony.

From Lieutenant-Colonel Browne's report, the conduct of the 28th Regiment was most praiseworthy during this service, which was rendered excessively fatiguing from the inclemency of the weather and length of the march;—this corresponds with the general conduct of that distinguished regiment.

By command,

*Guy Campbell*

M. S.

## The Battle of Barossa

1811. About the middle of February, an expedition was planned at Cadiz under the Spanish General La Pena, assisted by a British division under Sir Thomas Graham, to attack the French in rear of their lines, and to endeavour to raise the siege.

On the 23d of February, the Spanish army landed at Tariffa, accompanied by Sir Thomas Graham with a brigade of guards, the 67th, 87th, 95th (Rifles), the flank companies of the 47th, and 20th Portuguese, an admirable artillery under Colonel Dickson, and two squadrons of the 2nd German Hussars, under Major Busche. When the gallant general arrived at Tariffa, he found his old companion in arms, Colonel Browne, with "The Slashers," in such excellent order, that he obtained permission from General Campbell, for them to accompany him; we therefore formed a brigade with the 67th and 87th, under Colonel Wheatly of the guards. At that time Colonel Belson, returned from England, and re-assumed the command of the regiment; but the services of Colonel Browne were not forgotten;

the flank companies of the 9th and 82nd were sent from Gibraltar, and were formed with those of the 28th into a splendid flank battalion for him. The whole of the British were in the town of Tariffa; but the misery of that place was such, that every officer who arrived, on asking for an inn, was shown to the 28th's mess. Of course we were all happy to see them; but such was the number that dined with us, that a pipe of port was drunk in four days, although each individual was rigidly limited to a daily pint.

While were quartered in Tariffa, the garrison was reinforced by the Spanish regiment of Valencia, commanded by Colonel Baratel, without exception the finest fellow we had ever seen among the Spanish officers. One morning when he chanced to be on our parade, he was very much surprised to see our long drum with the arms of Valentia, and the number of his regiment upon it,—he inquired of Colonel Belson how we became possessed of it, who told him it was taken at Minorca in 1798; he acknowledged that it was an honourable trophy, and expressed himself glad to see it in such hands. This drum, however, was afterwards taken by the French, on the retreat from Salamanca.

On the 28th of February, the army left Tariffa, and on the first of March, on the approach of Colonel Browne's flank battalion, the French evacuated their post at Casa Vieja; we moved on the 2nd to Veger,—another post of the enemy; and in our progress had to cross a lake by a very narrow causeway. It was completely covered with water, about three feet deep; so that the men were obliged to wade; and if they had stepped a foot on either side, they would have been plunged into the lake. Here the conduct of Sir Thomas Graham, was truly praiseworthy, by the example he showed the men; for with his staff he remained dismounted in the water, pointing out the road until the whole column had passed.

The town of Veger, is situated on a very high sugar-loaf hill, whence the French could very easily see our movement. At two p m. on the 4th, the army advanced by the coast road by Conil, towards Cadiz; and at about twelve at noon, on the memorable 5th, after a cold and unpleasant night's march, we arrived on the slope of the Barossa height, where we halted;—our mess man being close up to us with plenty of prog, we all sat down and had an excellent breakfast, little suspecting how near we were to such hostile neighbours; after halting an hour we crossed the hill, and proceeded towards Cadiz. Colonel Browne's flankers remained on the look out.

We had not long left the heights, and were proceeding through a thick pine-wood, when a Spaniard galloped up to Sir Thomas at the head of the column, his horse covered with foam, and reported that the French were advancing;—a few shots in the rear confirmed his story. This was delightful news; for it is a remarkable fact that with British soldiers, after the longest and most fatiguing march, the instant they see an enemy, or hear a shot fired, they forget their fatigues and every hardship, and go into action as if they had not marched a mile.

The admirable decision of our gallant chief was the means of our gaining the day; he did not take time to counter-march the column, but went at once to the right about,—the men getting into their places on the march. As soon as we cleared the wood, we saw Colonel Browne's little band of heroes hard at it, keeping the enemy's left wing in check; the guards were in front, and they pushed forward in their usual gallant style to his support. As we disengaged ourselves from the wood, we formed line under cover of the 95th (Rifles), and advanced to meet their right wing, which was then coming down in close column; this gave us a great advantage, and here the coolness of Colonel Belson was conspicuous; we being the left regiment, he moved us up without firing a shot, close to their right battalion, which just began to deploy. Colonel Belson then gave orders to fire by platoons from centre to flanks, at the same time "to be sure to fire at their legs and spoil their dancing;"—this order was observed for a short time with dreadful effect The action now become general; twice did we attempt to charge the enemy, who being double our strength (our flank companies being away) only retired a little. Giving three cheers, we charged a third time, and succeeded— the enemy gave way, and fled in every direction; in less than two hours they had been beaten in every part of the field. God was pleased to grant to the British arms as glorious and complete a victory as ever was gained, having in our hands two generals, and five guns, besides two eagles as trophies,—a greater number of the enemy were killed, wounded, and taken prisoners, than the total amount of the British force when it entered the field of battle. We collected on the top of the hill, from which we had beaten the enemy, and saw the French retreating in great confusion towards Chiclana, dismayed and crest-fallen—we gave them three hearty British cheers, at parting.

We suffered much, both in officers and men. Lieutenant Bennet, of the light company, was killed, and Lieutenant Light, of the grenadiers, mortally wounded, Captain Mullins and Bradbey, Lieutenants Wilkinson, Moore and Anderson, were severely wounded, and Lieutenant Blakeney slightly. Our artillery, which was admirably served, made dreadful carnage in the ranks of the enemy. Marshal Victor, who commanded them, must have been rather disappointed, for it was told by some of the prisoners that he put new clothing on his army, in anticipation of a triumph, for he had made sure of beating the English. One of the battalions which suffered most was Colonel Browne's: their bravery cannot be too highly praised. When the enemy came within range of his gallant corps of flankers, he made them the following laconic speech: "There they are, you rascals, if you don't kill them, they will kill you; so fire away!"

Colonel Browne escaped in a wonderful manner; he was mounted on a large Spanish horse, and rode between the cross fire without any injury either to himself or his charger.

Our poor fellows rested a short time on the hill, after the termination of such a hard-fought action:—but what would Britons not do, when led by so gallant a chief! After a most harassing night's march, they had beaten a force of more than double their numbers, fresh from their snug quarters at Chiclana.

Hearing that we were to march to the Isla de Leon in the evening, I, accompanied by the late Lieutenant and Adjutant Bridgeland (then serjeant-major), went to that part of the field where Colonel Browne's flank battalion had so nobly fought, to look for the body of Lieutenant Bennet After a short search we found it The spectacle was truly horrible. A musket-ball had entered his forehead, and had carried away the whole of the back of the head: a portion of the brain was lying in his cap; still he breathed! The serjeant-major said he would never leave him as long as he had breath in his body; and perceiving the army moving down to the beach, on their way to the Isla, a force being left to cover the removal of the wounded, he tied up the shattered head, and placing the body on his shoulder, carried it four miles to the Bermuga Heights, where the army halted. The surgeon coming up, examined the body, and said that it was perfectly ridiculous to think of conveying it a yard further, for although breath remained, all feeling was past. We therefore procured two great coats, and in the most retired place we could find, placed one under and the other over our poor comrade, and with sore hearts left him. About twelve at night we crossed over to the Isla, and were glad to get under any sort of cover. Some of us found our way into a Spanish hospital, where we were fortunate enough to get some clean straw on which we could lie down, and repose our weary limbs.

About nine next morning I was aroused from a sound sleep by a soldier of the regiment He told me that a corpse had been brought in by some Spaniards, who said it was that of an English officer; upon which I instantly got up, and limped down stairs as well as I could, (for I had been wounded by a spent grape-shot about the middle of the action,[1]) when, shocking to relate, I saw the body of poor Bennet brought in a bread-bag. He was still breathing. The dust from the bread, which had almost filled his nostrils, mouth, and eyes, I quickly removed with a sponge and water. His usual placid smile was still upon his countenance; but no sooner had this last friendly office been performed, than our lamented comrade, with a deep sigh, expired.

The conduct of the two squadrons of the 2nd German Hussars was truly fine. It was a curious thing, that the French cavalry were in the same proportion to them that the infantry were to us,—more than double. They were led to the charge on the hill in the most gallant manner by Colonel the Hon. F. Ponsonby (now governor of Malta). Three times did they go through and through the ene-

---

1. About the middle of the action I was struck in the right thigh by a spent grape-shot, and was sent head over heels out of the ranks. For a short time I remained stunned, and a report was given out that I was killed, when Lieutenant Potter took the command of my company. However, I soon recovered, by the assistance of a fine old soldier of the name of Gough, my right-hand man, who had a canteen of water, (a precious thing at such a time,) which he poured upon my face, and in about ten minutes I was able to rejoin my company. On returning to the right, and touching Lieutenant Potter on the shoulder, it created in him no little astonishment to see me, as it were, arisen from the dead.

my, doing terrible execution, until they completely routed them. The hussars suffered a great loss in Captain Busche, who was mortally wounded, and died three days afterwards in the same hospital in which our wounded officers were placed, at the Isla de Leon. I shall never forget the night before this brave officer was buried. The whole of his men stood round the coffin in the deepest grief, saying they had lost their father; they sat up all the night singing hymns, the whole joining. It was the most touching scene of devotion that we had ever witnessed; it would have melted the stoutest heart. At the siege of Copenhagen, while we were under arms one morning, a little before sunrise, I remember this same regiment of Germans passing us. At first we could not conceive what delightful sounds were approaching, and to our surprise, we found it was the whole of them singing the morning hymn, led by the colonel!

One of the most severe wounds during this action was received by Captain Godwin, of the 9th, (since lieutenant-colonel, 41st,) belonging to Colonel Browne's flank battalion. He was cheering his men on, and in the act of waving his sword, when a musket-ball entered between the knuckles of his right hand, hitting the bone of the wrist, and sending fangs round it, as if it had been melted lead. He suffered dreadfully.

As I mentioned before, when we came out of the wood, we formed line under cover of the rifles, who retired by our flank as soon as we were ready to advance. One man, however still remained. He was called upon several times, and told that we were about to open our fire. We advanced,—no wonder he did not hear us;—we found him lying upon his belly, his rifle, on a stone, pointed at the enemy, his cheek on the butt. The rifle was cocked, and his finger on the trigger; but in the act of pulling it a musket ball had taken him in the head, and instantly deprived him of life.

One of our men took up the rifle, went down on his knees, and knocked down a Frenchman, to revenge, as he said, the fall of the brave rifleman. When we collected on the hill after the action, we all sat down to partake of what our haversacks afforded. Lieutenant Blakeney was rather astonished to find, on examination, that the musket ball which wounded him had almost spent itself in going through a ration-loaf and a roast fowl. I recollect also an old officer of the regiment—Captain Bowles—who went into action with a canteen of brandy over his shoulder, made fast under his sash—how he shrugged his shoulders, and longed for the water that had been sent for to have a glass of grog. When it came, to the mortification of all, on untying the canteen, he found that a shot had gone through it, and not a drop of the brandy was left.

During the action we saw nothing of the Spaniards under La Pena; but what was most extraordinary, two of their best regiments—the Walloon Guards, which were put into the brigade of guards, and the regiment Cuidad Real, in Colonel Wheatley's brigade—were somehow or other withdrawn from the British, and we did not see them again until they came up, when we were cheering on the top of the hill.

General orders issued by Sir Thomas Graham after the battle of Barossa:

> Isla
> March 6th, 1811
> The disadvantages under which the battle of yesterday was begun are so striking that it is unnecessary the Lieutenant-General should state to the troops that he considered the safety of the whole of the allied army (circumstanced as it was at the time) depended on our defeating the enemy. While he sincerely laments the sacrifice of the lives of so many gallant men, he trusts that it must be thought a necessary one.

The enemy's number and position were no longer objects of calculation, for there was no retreat; he confided in the known valour of the British troops, and his expectations were completely fulfilled. The fatigue of a night's march of sixteen hours was forgotten by every man in the division. When such unusual praise is due to the incomparable behaviour of all, it is impossible to particularize by name those who distinguished themselves. *All did.* He requests that Brigadier-General Dilkes and Colonel Wheatley will accept themselves, and convey to the commanding officers of the corps composing their respective brigades, and to all the officers of them, the assurance of his most grateful admiration of their conduct.

The same testimony of gratitude and high approbation is due to Lieutenant-Colonel Browne, 28th Regiment, and to Lieutenant-Colonel Barnard, 95th, commanding flank battalions; and to all the officers of the royal engineers; to Major Busche, 2nd Hussars, K.G.L. The intrepid charge made by a squadron of the hussars, headed by Captain Busche, attracted the notice of every one.

The Lieutenant-General's obligations to Lieutenant-Colonel Macdonald, the Honourable Lieutenant-Colonel Cathcart, and the officers of the quarter-master's and adjutant-general's departments, and to Captain Hope, and all the officers of his personal staff, for their exertions and assistance during the action, are deeply impressed on his mind.

The British troops saw with admiration how nobly the detachment of the 20th Portuguese upheld the character our allies have so fortunately established.

The Lieutenant-General requests that Major-General Whittingham and Captains Marenda and Frangton

> of the Spanish service, will accept his best thanks for their zeal and gallantry.
>
> The general of division, Rufin—the general of brigade, Rousseau—the eagle—and six pieces of artillery, are the trophies of the day.
>
> The loss of both sides, from the appearance of the field, must be severe. The different corps and detachments will send to the deputy adjutant-general as soon as possible the returns of killed, wounded, and missing, in the action of yesterday with the French *corps d'armée* commanded by Marshal Victor.

The regiment was quartered in casemates in the works of Cadiz. Most uncomfortably placed we were, both officers and men having nothing to keep us from the cold stones but our cloaks and blankets. We were employed on the outpost duties. On the 9th of March an attack was expected to take place on Pontales battery. A reinforcement of 100 men of the 28th under my command, accompanied by Lieutenants Robertson and Huddlestone, was ordered there at three in the afternoon. The distance was about two miles, and the only way we could go (unless by a most circuitous route) was along the seashore, exposed a good deal to the fire from the enemy's batteries at Matagorda; but going in Indian files at six paces, we reached the fort without having a man touched.

The fort was cannonaded the whole night; the Cadiz volunteers suffered severely; but from the excellent arrangements of Lieutenant Brett, Royal Artillery, the commandant (who was afterwards killed on the bridge of Seville), we did not lose a man. Next morning, after sunrise, every thing was quiet, and we found that no assault was to take place; we therefore returned to Cadiz in the same manner that we advanced, and with equally good fortune.

On the 12th, Pontales was again reinforced by 100 of

the 28th under Captain Bowles, Lieutenants Hartman and Coen, who were as fortunate as on the former occasion.

The 28th embarked at Cadiz on the 13th of March, and arrived at Gibraltar on the 16th. Sir Colin Campbell, the governor, was so pleased with the conduct of the regiment, that he ordered a *feu-de-joie* to be fired after dark on that evening, in commemoration of the battle of the 5th. We landed in a deplorable state—nothing but rags upon us; our clothing was very old when we commenced this short campaign, and the bullets of the French had torn it almost to pieces; there was hardly a cap that was not perforated. However, after we were all put to rights, we were not allowed to remain long idle.

On the 10th of July, we embarked on board two ships of war, and on the 21st landed at Lisbon to join the conqueror of the Peninsula, and the British army, in their glorious career. We there found two of our brother officers of the second battalion, Captain Carroll and Lieutenant Crummer[2], who had been severely wounded at the battle of Albuera on the 16th of May.

---

2. This officer, now Captain Crummer, and still in the regiment, was badly wounded in the left leg, and would not apply for a pension, to which he was entitled at the time; nor was he absent from the corps for a single day, except while under cure, during all their subsequent service abroad. In 1832, twenty-one years afterwards, whilst in quarters at Fermoy, his old wound broke out afresh, when several splinters of bone came away, so that he suffered more pain than at first On his recovery, he applied for the usual pension; but in consequence of the time he allowed to elapse, and the recent regulations of the service, his case could not be taken into consideration. I do not think there is such another leg in the United Kingdom without a pension.

## Chapter 5

# Third Campaign in the Peninsula

1811. After being perfectly equipped for the field, on the 2nd of August the 28th crossed the Tagus, and proceeded through the Alentejo to join General Hill's division. On the 10th we arrived at Villa Viciosa, where we found our second battalion, after an absence of six years; and on the 24th of August the men of the second were transferred to the first battalion.

The following extract from the general orders appeared on the occasion:

> The Commander of the Forces is concerned to part with Lieutenant-Colonel Abercrombie, and the officers and men of the second battalion 28th Regiment, with whose services he has had every reason to be satisfied; and he hopes he will have the benefit of their assistance in renewed strength.

Extract from the orders of Lieutenant-General Hill:

> The perfect discipline and soldier-like appearance of the second battalion of the 28th Regiment, and the zeal uniformly evinced by all ranks in it, have been so conspicuous, that Lieutenant-General Hill cannot allow Lieutenant-Colonel Abercrombie, his officers, and non-commissioned officers, to quit his command,

without expressing the very high sense he entertains of their past services, and the satisfaction which he shall derive from having them at some future period again placed under his orders.

The soldiers who are just drafted into the first battalion, have also the Lieutenant-General's best thanks for their exemplary conduct, and they will, he has no doubt, continue to deserve them.

On the 27th, the officers and non-commissioned officers of the second battalion commenced their march for Lisbon, to embark for England.

While we were quartered at Villa Viciosa, we suffered a great loss in Captain Russell, who was carried off by a fever when he had just succeeded to his company. He had been many years our adjutant, and was always looked upon as one of the best in the service: so much was he beloved by the whole regiment, that at his funeral not a dry eye could be seen among the men who had been under him. As a proof how he was esteemed by the soldiers, when we were upon service, if anything good was found by any foraging party, it usually found its way to poor Russell's tent

The regiment left Villa Viciosa on the 2nd of September, and arrived on the 5th at Portalegre, the head-quarters of General Hill, commanding the second division of Lord Wellington's army.

Colonel Abercrombie now returned from Lisbon, and assumed the command, Colonel Belson being obliged to go to England on account of ill health.

In consequence of a French *corps d'armée* under General Gerard, being observed in motion about the Spanish frontiers, on a foraging expedition, we expected a move.

On the 22nd of October, General Hill's division advanced from Portalegre, on the 23rd we crossed into Spain, and on the 26th, at daybreak, we arrived at Malpartida. To our great disappointment we found the enemy had left it but an hour before; they retired in the direction of Caceres; the 2nd Hussars came up, and skirmished with their rear-guard.

Here the consummate skill of our excellent commander showed itself. The French, on their arrival at Caceres, took the road to Merida by Arroyo del Molinos, where they halted on the 27th. On the same morning we left Malpartida by Aldea del Cano, and Casa de Don Antonio, a road parallel to that which the enemy had taken, but concealed from each other by a ridge of mountains.

After a very long forced march, in the most dreadful weather, we arrived in the afternoon at Alcuesca, about three miles from the spot where the French had halted. The light companies were thrown into the villages to prevent the natives from giving information to the enemy. The division (cavalry, artillery, and infantry), was formed in fields in the neighbourhood, with the strictest orders that not a fire was to be lighted for fear of apprising the French of our vicinity. A terrible stormy night, with strong wind, and abundance of rain, made our position truly miserable; our tents were all blown down, and we were obliged to lie under those wet covers without having anything warm to comfort us.

The arrangements our general made were excellent; at one in the morning the different columns fell in without a drum or a bugle sounding. We filed through the village, and crossed the mountain. A little before daybreak, the division formed under a rising ground within half a mile of Arroyo, amidst a dreadful storm of hail, which, fortunately for us, was at our backs, and consequently in the faces of the French videttes, who turned their backs to it.

We were soon formed: the anxiety and delight of the army were wound up to the utmost pitch, when we found the bird had not flown, but still remained in fancied security in the village; it seemed as though fortune had determined to favour us, for just as we were ready to move, the weather cleared up, and gave us a full view of the first brigade, consisting of the 50th, and 71st and 92nd, moving directly on the village. The gallant Highlanders, Cameron leading the advance, marched into the town, the pipes playing "Heigh, Johnny Cope, are you waking yet?"—the second brigade, 28th, 34th, and 39th, under General Howard, moved round and got to the other side of the village to meet them. The first brigade found the enemy preparing to march, and drove them out in the most gallant manner.

The French, completely taken by surprise, endeavoured to form on the Merida side; but seeing our brigade rapidly advancing upon them, and the 71st skirmishing through the gardens in their rear, after a few rounds from the Portuguese guns, which did considerable execution, they broke, and took to the mountains on their left, throwing away their arms, and climbing the heights in every direction. The 28th and 34th instantly pursued, the 39th going round to endeavour to intercept them. We took a great many prisoners. The weather was very fine, and it was a most gratifying sight for us to see the enemy scampering up the mountain in every direction; the British, notwithstanding the forced march the day before, being in wet jackets for twenty-four hours, and the night's march before the attack, were taking them at every step. On our arrival at the summit, our men were very much scattered, and General Howard most judiciously stopped the pursuit. At this period our gallant comrade, Captain Irving (now Lieutenant-Colonel), fell senseless from fatigue and exhaustion, and it was with great difficulty he was restored. Seven or eight Frenchmen, whilst endeavouring to make their escape down the mountain, were taken in an extraordinary manner by Lieutenant Irwin, of the grenadier company, the first in the pursuit He took up what they call in Ireland a couple of "two-year-old stones,"[3] which he aimed so well with his *left hand,* that he brought down two of the Frenchmen, one after the other; the others seeing their comrades so roughly handled, quietly surrendered, and he brought them all in prisoners. On our descent into the plain, the scene was a singular one; many officers and soldiers were mounted on horses they had picked up belonging to French officers, who finding they could not ride over the mountain, had abandoned them; and different parties were bringing in numerous prisoners, which, when collected, amounted to upwards of 1500: the Prince D'Aremberg, General Brune, and several officers of rank, were amongst them. The Prince D'Aremberg was taken by Lieutenant Blakeney, of the light company, 28th, who being mounted, as adjutant of the flankers, was at the head of the column. On coming up to a wall where a number of French officers had just retreated, seeing a person of distinction, with a star upon his breast, he gallantly leaped the wall into the midst, and made the prince his prisoner.

The Prince was so much pleased with the conduct of Lieutenant Blakeney, that he applied to General Hill to permit the Lieutenant to conduct him to Lisbon, which was granted;—he was promoted to a company in the 36th for his bravery. When it was made known to the Prince that the frigate was ready, which was appointed to take him to England, he told Blakeney that he should be happy to see him, whenever he might be at Brussels, Paris, Rome, Naples, or in any part of the Emperor's dominions. A midshipman soon after came to say that a boat was waiting, when the Prince turned to Blakeney, and asked

3. About the size of a man's hand.

him how soon he thought he (the Prince) should be in England. Blakeney replied, "As soon as you are out of the Tagus —all the seas are England."

The enemy's artillery, consisting of four pieces, had just commenced their march for Merida, before the attack; they were perceived by General Howard, as our brigade crossed the plain, and he ordered the light companies of the 28th, 34th and 39th, to dash across some vineyards to gain the Merida road before them;— assisted by the cavalry, they rushed upon them in the most gallant manner; the French had only time to unlimber, but not to fire a shot, when they were all taken.

At the foot of the mountain where the enemy were broken, many of the French officers came up to the British officers, with their purses and watches in their hands, requesting we would take care of them, for fear they should be taken by the men; of course, they were all faithfully returned to the poor fellows when the affair was over.

After this brilliant surprise, our fatigues and hardships were forgotten; our brigade took possession of Arroyo del Molinos, and the 1st proceeded to Merida. The afternoon was employed in collecting the wounded French, who were very numerous: the British loss was trifling.

The spirited conduct of Lieutenant-Colonel Lindsay, commanding the 39th, deserves to be mentioned. It has been already stated, they were sent round the mountain to endeavour to intercept the French. Gerard, with about 500 men escaped by Sierra Montanches. To hasten their flight, many threw away their packs and appointments; but the 39th, by an extraordinary rapid march, came up to their rear-guard, which occasionally took up a position to cover the retreat. After some skirmishing, the French descended into the plain; but the 39th were so fatigued by a harassing march from two in the morning till six in the evening, that Colonel Lindsay, finding it impossible to get the men farther, had recourse to a *ruse-de-guerre.* He rode up to the French rear-guard with a flag of truce, and proposed to Gerard to surrender, stating that he would be "intercepted by the British cavalry in the plain, and by Morillo's corps in the mountains." A captain and about twenty men gave themselves up; but mortified at the loss of his corps, the French general, having in his hands a brace of pistols, declared nobly that he would sooner die than surrender; he then with a handful of men escaped by the bridge of Medellin, and the 39th joined the brigade next morning at Arroyo del Molinos. Our friends the 34th got a capital supply of drums in this affair, having taken the whole belonging to the 34th French regiment

Next day, the 29th, the 2nd brigade being joined by the 39th with the prisoners, returned to Alcuesca. Many of the unfortunate French were so badly wounded that they could not be moved; we were therefore obliged to leave them in the village, when we marched. It was truly heart-rending to hear their cries, and many requested, we would shoot them, rather than leave them to the mercy of the Spaniards. No doubt, after our departure, the stiletto put an end to their sufferings.

On the 31st of October the 2nd brigade reached Albuquerque, where we were cantoned. A lamentable affair happened whilst we were quartered there. Two of the handsomest men of the light company, M'Cann and Ludley, were billeted in a house containing a mother and her daughter, when one evening a Spaniard came in and invited them to take some wine with him, during which, it is supposed, in a fit of jealousy, he took the opportunity of stabbing them both to the heart! The assassin made his escape before the alarm could be given, as also did the mother and daughter; but our men were so exasperated that they attacked the house, and in twenty minutes there was not one stone left upon another. The 3rd brigade proceeded with their prisoners to Portalegre, and we remained at Albuquerque, until the end of December.

On Christmas day, while we were all snug at our dinners, we received a hint that we were about to advance, by the unexpected arrival of the Marquis of Tweeddale, on the quartermaster general's staff, who came to prepare quarters for the second division in this miserable town. The 2nd division, having collected on the 28th, we again advanced, and bivouacked half way to Merida. On the morning of the 29th, as we were passing the village of La Nava, our advanced guard of cavalry fell in with a foraging party of 300 French voltigeurs, under the command of Captain Neville. They were attacked by part of the cavalry of the division; and after every attempt to break their square, this brave Frenchman conducted his little gallant band safely into Merida, even carrying away his wounded.

Next day, the 30th, we reached Merida. On the march we saw two Frenchmen lying on the road; they had been killed by Captain Maxwell's guns, which having been brought up, fired a few rounds at the end of the affair. The French happened to have a few hussars with them, who gave the alarm at the approach of the British, or we should have had another surprise. We heard that Captain Neville was promoted for his gallant conduct

1812. On the 1st of January the division marched to Almendralejo, expecting to come up with the Count D'Erlon, who, however, retired towards Villa Franca in considerable haste when he heard of our approach.

On the 3rd January Sir Rowland sent Colonel Abercrombie with a force, consisting of the 28th Regiment, the 20th Portuguese Cavalry, and a troop of the 2nd German Hussars, to endeavour to intercept a strong reconnoitring party of the enemy's cavalry. We advanced to Fuentes del Maestre, about four leagues, when Colonel Abercrombie received information that a strong French patrol was advancing on the Los Santos road, perfectly unconscious of being so near the British. Colonel Abercrombie instantly decided upon attacking them. The hussars and Portuguese cavalry were formed upon the road; the flank companies, 28th, on a hill to the left; and the remainder of the regiment in column in the town, ready to act at a moment's notice—all perfectly concealed from the enemy. The admirable dispositions of our gallant leader proved that he was a worthy son of the conqueror of Egypt. The moment the French showed round the hill the little force gave three British cheers, when Colonel Abercrombie gallantly charged at the head of the cavalry, while the light company attacked their right. In a very few minutes the French were completely routed, leaving several dead, and two officers, and about thirty wounded and prisoners. The 2nd Hussars behaved in their usual style. The Portuguese were nobly led by Colonel Campbell and Lieutenant, (now Lord) Hutchinson. The French force consisted of a strong detachment of mounted grenadiers, sent out from Los Santos to *feel* us, which they certainly did. The hussars had one rank and file and two horses killed; two sergeants, twelve rank and file, and four horses wounded. The Portuguese cavalry, one staff, five rank and file, one horse wounded, and one horse missing. The prisoners were sent into Almandralejo that night, the troops remaining in a neighbouring olive wood, where we suffered severely from the cold and rain, and retired in the morning.

On the 5th the division returned to Merida, in consequence of the investment of Cuidad Rodrigo. Sir Rowland commenced his march by Portalegre, to Niza, to cover it. On the first day's march, when we passed the place where the two Frenchmen of Captain Neville's gallant party were killed by the cannon shot on the 29th, it was curious to observe that one body was completely devoured by the wolves—even the very gristles of the ribs were gnawed off; while the other was not touched, nor even were his clothes in the smallest degree injured.

We remained at Niza till after the storming of Cuidad Rodrigo; and having seen the prisoners pass on their way to Lisbon, the division moved to Portalegre, and our brigade returned to Albuquerque. Badajos being about to be besieged, about the middle of March we moved with the second division to Merida, where the 13th Dragoons took a few prisoners.

On the 16th Badajos was invested, when we advanced to Almendralejo, and on the 27th moved to Medellin. Soult, having now collected all the troops he could, and being joined by the Count D'Erlon, advanced to Usagre. The division returned to Merida, where we crossed the Guadiana, and blew up an arch of that beautiful old Roman bridge of sixty-four arches. We then moved on to Talavera del Re, about three miles from Badajos, and covered the storm of the memorable night of the 6th April. With anxious eyes did we look on at that awful scene. The firing died away towards morning, when we were delighted to find our gallant fellows had succeeded in that terrible contest. We had three captains on the staff, one of whom was killed—Captain James Johnson, *aid-de-camp* to Major-General Bowes, while gallantly leading a column to the breach, received a musket-shot through the thigh, and as he was carried to the rear, cheering the men as they passed him, was killed by a grape-shot. Captain Potter, an old and excellent officer, brigade-major in the 4th division, had his right leg so dreadfully wounded, that he died after, undergoing amputation. Major Stovin, on the staff of the third division, escaped.

He was one of the gallant leaders in escalading the castle. Lieutenant Huddlestone, of the regiment, was also there, as acting engineer, and behaved in the most intrepid manner, in heading the column, and placing the ladders at the castle walls. He received the warmest thanks of Colonel Fletcher, the chief engineer. Soult, finding he could not save Badajos, retired, when we advanced, and were again quartered at Almendralejo.

On the 12th Sir Rowland left Almendralejo with the first and second brigades, and Colonel Ashworth's Portuguese, on a well-arranged expedition—the destruction of the bridge across the Tagus at Almaraz. Three days' soft bread was served out to us before we commenced the march.[4]

We moved by Medellin and Truxillo (the birth-place of the famous Pizarro), and arrived at Jarraicejo on the morning of the 16th. On the same afternoon we were practised in scaling a dry bridge with ladders which had been used at Badajos a little more than a month before. They were covered with blood and brains!

The same evening we moved off in three columns,—the right, 50th, 71st, and 92nd, under Major-General Howard; and the left, 28th, 34th, and 4th Caçadores, under Major-General Chowne,—were to endeavour to surprise the castle of Marabita. The centre—the 6th and 18th Portuguese, and 13th Dragoons—under Major-General Long.

The departure of the columns was an interesting and impressive sight to us. The forlorn hope, destined to lead the attack on the castle, was commanded by a fine fellow, Lieutenant Sullivan, of the 34th, and was composed of volunteers from that corps, the 28th, and 39th, the grenadiers

4. The following advice was given by a fine old soldier to his young comrades on one of these occasions: "An old soldier well knows the value of a good *tommy* (a loaf of bread), and he ought to instil into the mind of the young soldier how necessary it is to take the greatest care of it, and not to devour in one day what is intended to last for three."

of the 28th, under Lieutenants Irwin and Hilliard, and supported by the light company of the 28th; the whole under Major Mullins. Next to them followed a party under Lieutenant Coen, with scaling-ladders and petards; then came the pioneers with crow-bars and pickaxes; after which the column advanced, with arms secured. An order had been issued that not a word was to be spoken, lest the peasantry should hear us, and give information. Nothing was therefore heard but the tramp of the men. We traversed the woods the whole night by goat-paths; but unfortunately for our column, from the circuitous and bad road we had to go, we did not reach the bottom of the hill until daylight, which exposed us to the view of the enemy, who instantly commenced a cannonade. The forlorn hope and light companies, under Captain Bradbey, pushed rapidly up the hill, and down on all their out-posts, when it was found the castle was too strong to be taken by surprise. The columns retired out of the range of shot, and the flankers were withdrawn in the evening.

The road to the bridge of Almaraz being still commanded by the castle, on the night of the 18th Sir Rowland Hill, with the brigade under the command of General Howard, went by a circuitous course to the right, and on the morning of the 19th made a most gallant attack on Fort Napoleon, which covered the bridge. It was nobly carried under a fire of grape from eighteen pieces of cannon, by the 50th and 71st, supported by the 92nd, but with a severe loss. The enemy flying from it to the *Tête du Pont*, the gallant Highlanders dashed forward, and entered with them. The commander of Fort Ragusa, on the opposite bank of the Tagus, being seized with a panic, had cut away the bridge of boats. Many of his countrymen were consequently either drowned or made prisoners. The attention of all was now directed to the passage of the river, when some of the 92nd immediately leaped in, and swam to the opposite side, bringing the boats back with them. Sir Rowland was so struck with the conduct of James Gould and Walter Somerville, the two first of the grenadiers who swam the river, that he gave them two ounces of gold each upon their return with the boats. Thus was the bridge secured with Fort Ragusa, which the enemy immediately abandoned. During this gallant affair a false attack was made on the castle by the flankers of the left column under Captain Bradbey, supported by the 28th and 34th, which completely succeeded in drawing off their attention during the storming of the fort. In this affair we had only two men wounded. An excellent officer, Captain Chandler of the 50th, in bravely leading his men up the ladders, had his head carried off by a cannon shot. Sir Rowland having accomplished the object of the expedition—the complete destruction of the bridge and fort—we retired by the same route to our cantonments at Almendralejo. This brilliant *coup-de-main* cut off the communication between Marmont and Soult.

CHAPTER 6

# Advance to Aranguez and Madrid

Soult, having now been joined by the Count D'Erlon, again advanced in great force. Sir Rowland, calling in all his out-posts, retired, and in a masterly style, on the 18th June, took up the old position of Albuera, waiting to receive the enemy, who had now occupied Santa Martha, Fuentes del Maestre, and Almendralejo.

The field of Albuera was most interesting to us, our second battalion having fought so bravely in that memorable battle the year before. We found many remains of the fine fellows who had fallen. For some days the two armies remained quietly looking at each other, as though waiting to see who would strike the first blow.

On the 3rd of July the French advanced to Villa Gracia, and on the 9th some skirmishing took place. On the 13th a few Polish lancers deserted to us, and the two armies remained quiet until the 24th, when there was an affair of cavalry, in which the French were beaten in the most gallant style.

On the afternoon of the 28th, 300 of the enemy's cavalry dashed into the wood of Albuera, and sabred three or four of a picquet of the 3rd Dragoon Guards. Our bivouac being nearest, Colonel Abercrombie, at the head of the 28th, ran to their assistance, supported by the 34th and 39th; but we were too late—the enemy had retired.

On the morning of the 29th, Soult, perhaps apprehending he should be served as he had been the year before at the same place, retreated by Los Santos and Zafra. On the 5th of July we advanced, and bivouacked near Bienvenida; and on the 7th we again advanced to Llerena, famed for the gallant attack made by Sir Stapleton Cotton, with two brigades of cavalry, on 2,500 of the enemy, which were defeated with great loss. We remained a few days, and went into cantonments at Zafra, where we remained until the middle of August, when we advanced to Huerta, to endeavour to fall in with Drouet. In the beginning of September, we moved with the second division by Don Benito, to Medellin, and on the 14th we again entered Truxillo. Between Don Benito and Medellin, we crossed that bloody field of battle where a Spanish army, under Cuestra, had been entirely cut to pieces by a French corps under Victor, on the 28th of March, 1809. The plain was completely covered with their blanched bones. A story is told, that Victor ordered a certain quantity of spirits to be issued to his dragoons to bathe their wrists after that dreadful slaughter. We crossed the Tagus at Almaraz on the 16th, and on that day passed the castle of Marabita, which we had endeavoured to surprise on the morning of the 17th of May. It had lately been evacuated by the French, and we found, on examination, that it would have been quite impossible to escalade it; for besides the outworks, it consisted of an immense circular tower, with a door half-way up, out of the reach of any ladder.

We moved by Naval Moral, Orapesa, and Talavera, and on the 1st of October we reached Toledo. At Talavera, where we halted a day, we had an opportunity of visiting that field of one of the first and most glorious achievements of our great commander. The field was shown to us by Lieutenant Irwin, of the grenadier company, who shared in the glories of that ever-memorable battle, with the first battalion of detachments. We found several remnants of the clothes of our poor fellows who had fallen there. We also visited the grave of that gallant fellow, Lieutenant-Colonel Gordon, of the 83rd Regiment. On the 2nd of October, we left Toledo, and moved to Yepes and Aranguez, where the second division was cantoned.[1]

Soult having collected a strong force, we retired on the 30th of October, from the position of the Jarama, after destroying the bridge of Aranguez. In the afternoon an attempt was made to destroy the Puente Largo, but the mine failed; and the enemy pushed forward a strong force to endeavour to get possession of it. At that moment, the second battalion 47th, and part of the rifles arrived, under Colonel Skerrett, on their march from Cadiz; they attacked the French, and gallantly drove them back. We continued our march that night in the direction of Madrid, which we passed next morning, and having halted to cover the destruction of some stores, we continued our march, and on the 3rd of November, we joined Lord Wellington at Adeja, on his memorable retreat from Burgos.

The troops under the command of Sir Rowland Hill, crossed the Tormes, at Alba, on the 8th. Major-General Howard's brigade was left at Alba, the remainder was posted at the Fords of Encinas and Huerta.

Whilst we were on the march about four miles from Alba, Lieutenant Irwin, of the grenadiers, had a singular op-

---

1. On one of the marches between Toledo and Yepes, when we were much in advance of our baggage, and greatly in want of food, Major Ross, of the 4th Dragoon Guards (now Colonel Ross), was passing at the head of his regiment, and having a large piece of roast beef on his holsters, off which he had just lunched, and seeing us looking rather hungry, he took up the beef, and calling out "Ch——ie, there is an old saying in Scotland, hit a hungry dog with a bone, you won't hurt him;" at the same time throwing the beef. It is needless to say, it was very soon disposed of amongst us, without waiting for bread or salt.

portunity of displaying his personal strength and intrepidity. An over-driven bullock got among the ranks of the regiment, and was knocking the men about very unceremoniously, when Lieutenant Irwin rushed forward, and boldly seizing the animal by the horns, actually threw him over upon his back into a deep cut in the road, where he was instantly killed, and cut up by the hungry soldiers; nor was he then done with, for we left a party to cut up the hide into sandals for some of the men who had lost their shoes.

On the 9th, the enemy drove in the picquets in front of Alba, with a strong force of infantry, and with twenty pieces of cannon began to cannonade the town: the brave 50th, 71st, and 92nd defended it, against all the efforts of the French, who withdrew in the night.

During the 10th, 11th, 12th, and 13th, we were still anxiously watching the different fords: upon the 14th, the enemy crossed the Tormes two leagues above Alba. The second division, with a strong force of cavalry, moved in their direction; and in the afternoon our artillery opened a heavy cannonade upon them, but without bringing on an action. That night we bivouacked in a wood adjacent to the field of Salamanca, where the great battle was fought on the 22nd of July. We found the skeletons of many unfortunate wounded Frenchmen, who had crawled there to protect themselves from the scorching rays of the sun. It was evident the French did not like to fight us on the old ground; next morning, therefore—the 10th— we moved in the direction of Cuidad Rodrigo.

On the 17th, our march became very harassing: the enemy followed us with a strong force of cavalry, and the mule, with all the books and documents of the regiment, fell into their hands; likewise the long drum, which had been taken from the Spaniards at Minorca. In the afternoon, after crossing a narrow plain to a wood, where we were to bivouack for the night, and just as the regiment was dismissed, a large body of the enemy's Polish Lancers made their appearance, and after shamefully cutting down several unfortunate women, who had fallen behind, advanced rapidly to the wood, where we were stationed. The light-company fortunately happened to be on the rear-guard, under Captain Bradbey; and they instantly formed at the edge of the wood, and gave them such a well directed volley, that many of them were brought down. The regiment then formed into square as quickly as possible, and the 14th Light Dragoons, with a part of the 1st Hussars, under Colonel Hervey, coming up, attacked and completely defeated them, killing and wounding a great many, and taking a considerable number prisoners. Twice did we lose our frugal meal, that afternoon,—being obliged to fall in, and form square, to resist the enemy.

We had a most harassing march this day through a woody country, and the army suffered a severe loss in Sir Edward Paget, who was taken by a patrol of the enemy, in a wood between the 5th and 7th divisions. That afternoon, the enemy's advanced guard came up with the light division, and cannonaded them from a height, as they crossed the Huebra, at San Munoz, on which occasion an excellent officer, Captain Dawson, of the 52nd, was killed: we had just bivouacked in a wood, fortunately out of range of their guns. After having crossed, we fell in and prepared for action; but the French did not attempt to leave the heights. This was the last time they annoyed us on the retreat

On the 18th, the troops suffered much from the stupidity of the guides—fording so many rivers that were much swollen from the heavy rains that had fallen. On the 19th, we crossed the Agueda.

On this short but severe retreat we suffered many hardships from the inclemency of the weather; and as from the badness of the roads our supplies could not come up to us for two or three days, the acorns of the cork-oak were our principal food. Wheat was served out to us when it could be got, which we pounded between two stones and boiled; pork was now and then to be had, but having no salt, we could not make use of it. We were quartered for several days in the village of Santiago, with a part of the 4th Dragoon Guards, whence we crossed the Sierra de Gata, passing the villages of Gata, and Noroligo. At the end of November, Sir Rowland Hill's corps was cantoned in Casa de Gomez; and other villages in the neighbourhood of Coria. During this retreat we lost Lieutenant Charles Huddlestone, who had never perfectly recovered from the fatigue he underwent at the siege of Badajos; and he suffered so much from the cold and wet, that he was sent to the rear, and actually died on his horse, within a short distance of Lisbon.

1813. At the end of January, we lost a gallant officer, by the death of our Brigadier-General Wilson, who was succeeded by the Hon. Colonel O'Callaghan, of the 39th Regiment.

On the 5th of February, we moved to Coria[2], the head-quarters of the corps, and here joined the other two regiments of the brigade, the 34th and 39th[3].

---

2. While we were in winter quarters round Coria, Brevet Lieutenant-Colonel Paterson, 28th Regiment, being sent to the rear to bring up the efficient men out of hospital, was riding on his return with Captain Egerton, of the 34th Regiment, (now Colonel and *Aid-de-camp* to Lord Hill.) they observed some vultures eating the carcase of a horse. Having alighted, to take a nearer view, Colonel Paterson drew his sabre, and gave one of them who was gorged so hard a blow, that the blade broke in two; Captain Egerton laid hold of the wing, when the creature,having disgorged himself, to their astonishment flew away, leaving behind in Captain Egerton's hands only a large feather, which he wore in his hat as a trophy when he came up to the division.

3. The quartermaster general's staff of the 2nd division about this time had to regret the loss of that active officer, the Marquis of Tweeddale, who generally led the advance; he was appointed to command the 100th Regiment, in America, and was severely wounded at their head on the 5th July, 1814.

On the recall of Marshal Soult to Germany, to the assistance of Napoleon, he is said to have given the following piece of advice to his successor:

> Whenever you find the British army in retreat, let them alone, and they will go to the devil their own way; but if you go near them, they will get into their places, and give you such a drubbing as you never had before.

## Chapter 7

# Vittoria and the Pyrenees

Colonel Belson, having returned from England, re-assumed the command of the regiment, and Colonel Abercrombie was appointed to the staff of the 6th division.

Coria is situated in a most fertile country—during our stay there, our winter amusements were coursing and shooting; we likewise got up an excellent theatre, and were as happy as possible, Sir Rowland doing everything in his power to add to our amusements. We remained in comfortable quarters until the 25th of April, when we marched to Torregoncillo, and on the 4th of May, we moved to Galisteo; at this place the whole of Sir Rowland's corps having concentrated, we encamped. On the 16th, being the second anniversary of the battle of Albuera, the regiment gave a dinner to Sir Rowland Hill, and the staff of the 2nd division. Being encamped, we had no tables or chairs, but the deficiency was ingeniously supplied by Lieutenant Irwin. A nice piece of turf being selected, he marked out the length and breadth of a mess table, for a hundred covers. The sward was carefully lifted, and a trench dug round large enough to accommodate the party; the sods and mould were then carefully placed in the centre, and levelled,—this centre-piece was excavated sufficiently to give room for our legs underneath: when the mass was raised to a proper height, the sward was carefully laid on, so that we had a beautiful green table, novel and ingenious. The dinner was cooked in every way the old soldier could invent—roast and boiled—soup and *bouillé*:—camp kettles were reversed for ovens to bake pies, and every guest brought his knife, fork, and plate. The wine of the country being excellent, we all enjoyed ourselves much; so much so, that some of us bivouacked under the table for the night.

On the 20th we were reviewed by Sir Rowland, and on the 21st we commenced our march by Villa Nueva, Aldea Nueva, and Banos, leaving Bejar to our right, where the 50th, under Colonel Harrison, and the 6th Caçadores, under Major Mitchell, had so gallantly repulsed a French division under General Foy, on the 20th of February preceding. The day we passed Banos the brigade suffered a severe loss in Captain Darly, commanding the light company of the 39th regiment, who, about half an hour after we got into our bivouack, burst a blood vessel, and died instantly. After a delightful march we arrived at Salamanca, on the 26th.

On this march we crossed some immense plains, and not being in the presence of the enemy, Sir Rowland Hill, indulged such of the officers who had greyhounds, with permission to course the hares alongside the columns,—this sport beguiled many a weary league to both officers and men, besides furnishing a good addition to our miserable pound of ration beef. It often happened that the hares made for, and were killed in the columns. We generally kept clear of the towns; for we were now well supplied with provisions by our excellent Commissary General Brooke, and the nightly bivouack was formed where there was plenty of wood and water. The French retired on our approach, but were overtaken by the British cavalry under Generals Fane and Alton, who killed many, and took 200 prisoners.

We remained encamped on the banks of the Tormes for

some days; some of the enemy were, however, still hovering about, and the following hint was given by Sir William Stewart, to the officers:

> Camp, near Oblada
> 30th May, 1813
> D. O.
> As a force of the enemy's cavalry are in the neighbourhood of the camp, the Lieutenant-General wishes the officers of the corps not to go out.

Sir Rowland's corps moved forward in the beginning of June, and on the 4th crossed the Douro at Toro (where the two brothers, Lord Paget and Sir Edward, had met on the 12th December, 1808, on the advance of Sir John Moore). With difficulty we passed the bridge over planks, the French having almost destroyed it. The river was very rapid, and our baggage animals being obliged to ford it, the baggage was in some danger; but by the assistance of the cavalry it was brought safely over.

We moved forward again on the 4th, and advanced rapidly to the neighbourhood of Burgos. On the 12th Lord Wellington marched, with Sir R. Hill's corps and a large body of cavalry, to Hermaza, where a considerable force of the enemy was posted on the heights. The cavalry turned their right: the second brigade, (28th, 34th, and 39th,) under the Hon. Colonel O'Callaghan, then moved up the heights from the village; but the enemy did not retire until we got almost within shot of them.

We advanced rapidly under the gallant Colonel O'Callaghan; and just as we had mounted the hill, and expected to go into action, we found, to our disappointment, an immense ravine separated us from the enemy. Their right being turned, they retired so rapidly, that we could not come up with them; but were obliged to look on while the cavalry and Major Gardener's horse artillery attacked them most gallantly. A squadron of the 14th Dragoons, under Captain Miles, took a gun and some prisoners before they could pass the Arlanza. In the evening the brigade retired to the village, leaving a strong picquet of the 28th on the heights.

About one o'clock, on the morning of the 13th, we were aroused by a dreadful explosion; but when day broke we were delighted to find that it was the destruction of the castle of Burgos, which had been blown up by the enemy, and before which so much British blood had been spilt the year before. Next morning we moved to the left, leaving Burgos on our right, and soon after passed the Ebro at Miranda. Nothing of any consequence occurred till the afternoon of thc 20th. Sir Rowland's corps took up its station on the right of the allied army, upon the Zadorra, we—the 28th—little suspecting that the French army was so near us in the position at Vittoria. Early on the morning of the memorable 21st, some of us were recommended by a staff officer "to get our breakfasts, and have our baggage packed as soon as possible."

There was an unusual scene of bustle in the bivouack; but what most convinced us that some work was to be done, was when we saw the favourite black charger, fully caparisoned, of our chief, Sir Rowland, (who was always as cool in action as on a field-day,) and the chestnut of Sir William Stewart, the brave leader of the British division of Hill's corps[1], whose soldier-like manner, when calmly, in the hottest fire, giving his orders, with his usual lisp, and gently switching the mane of his horse with a white cane, must be well remembered by all who served under him. About

1. Sir Rowland's corps, in this memorable campaign, was composed of a British division of three brigades, a Portuguese division of two brigades, a division of cavalry of two brigades, one heavy and the other light, with a powerful artillery.

nine, a.m. we moved, and crossed the Zadorra at La Puebla, when the skirmishing of the Spaniards, under Morillo, and the 71st, under Colonel Cadogan, was heard on the heights on the left of the enemy's position. We moved on at double quick for about a league, until we passed the defile formed by the heights and the river, which opened to our view the magnificent sight of the French army drawn up in battle array, with the spire of Vittoria behind them. Our brigade, under Colonel O'Callaghan, after being allowed a short breathing time, wheeled to the right, attacked, and drove the enemy from the village Sabijana de Alava, which we kept during the whole action against the many desperate attempts that they made to regain it. About four in the afternoon, the French army, being routed on their centre, and turned on their right, withdrew a large part of their force that was opposed to us, when we advanced, and drove what remained before us over the heights in our front. The sight was then beautiful—the enemy flying towards Vittoria, followed by the British and Portuguese. From the strong and difficult ground we had to cross, so intercepted by deep ravines caused by the mountain torrents, our brigade was much scattered. When we formed, we moved down along the hills to the right of the town, and bivouacked for the night on the height, about two miles beyond it.

In the glorious battle of Vittoria (where a British army had been victorious centuries ago) we suffered much. One serjeant and eleven rank and file killed; one major, two captains, twelve lieutenants, two ensigns, six serjeants, and 165 rank and file, wounded. Four officers died of their wounds, *viz.* Brevet Lieutenant-Colonel Paterson, (of the Castle Huntley family,) who was an excellent officer, and much regretted; and three fine young men, Lieutenants M'Donald, Mitchell, and Byrne. Soon after we had taken the village of Sabijana, the regiment formed in close column upon a gentle slope, and the men were ordered to go to the right about and sit down, resting their backs on their packs. We had remained but a few minutes in this situation when the enemy brought two guns to bear upon us. The second or third round struck a man of the name of M'Donell, of Captain Irving's company, on the back of the head, which it shattered in pieces over the regiment, wounding two other men. The body of poor M'Donell, who was sitting close to Captain Irving, never moved; his firelock rested on his breast between his clasped hands; the fingers gently dropped, leaving the thumbs supporting it. Soon after this we were sent out by companies, and skirmished the whole day[2].

List of Officers wounded at the battle of Vittoria

**Severely**
Brevet Lieut.-Col. Patterson; *died*
Captain Wilson
Captain Bowles
Lieutenant Wolf
Lieutenant Morris
Lieutenant Irwin
Lieutenant Sweeny
Lieutenant McDonnell; *died*
Lieutenant Burn
Lieutenant R. Mitchell
Lieutenant R. H. Mitchell; *died*
Ensign Burn; *died*

**Slightly**
Lieutenant Gordon
Lieutenant Coen
Lieutenant Clark
Lieutenant Evans
Ensign Alexander

Directly in front of the village which we defended there was a thick olive wood; we had a number of men knocked down, and could not see where the fire came from. At last

2. A little anecdote must here be allowed to be recorded of an Irishman, Dan. Fitzgibbon, of the grenadiers, who, like most of his countrymen, possessed both courage and humour. He was placed at a bank, which he was to fire over; but was told on no account to show himself. Poor Dan, not taking this advice, jumped upon the bank every round he fired, to see if he had hit any one. At last, a Frenchman shot him through the back of the left hand. It was seen that something had happened, and he was asked what was the matter? Dan, very quietly looking at his bleeding fist, and scratching his head with the other, said, "I wish I knew who did this."

a Frenchman was seen to fall out of one of the trees, which explained the mystery. At this time our ammunition having failed us, we were anxiously waiting for a supply, which, however, soon arriving, we instantly opened a sharp fire into the thickest part of the wood, which brought them down in great numbers.

The French army having been turned off the main road to France by the division under Sir T. Graham, retreated in the most precipitate manner towards Pampeluna, followed by Sir Rowland. The two first days we passed a great many of the enemy lying by the sides of the road, who had died of their wounds.

An awful accident happened to us on the afternoon of the 24th, as we were getting to our bivouac, near a village occupied by the 5th Dragoon Guards. At the moment when the adjutants of the brigade were called to take up their ground, a thunder-storm burst over our heads. A fine gallant fellow, Lieutenant and Adjutant Masterman, of the 34th, was coming from the rear, and was just abreast of the right centre company of the 28th, when the electric fluid struck him on the head, and passing down through his body, killed both man and horse. Poor Masterman's body instantly turned as black as if it had been burnt. Four men of No. 4 company were also struck down, and rendered unfit for the service; and the shock was so great, that two or three of our officers, who were in conversation at the time with some of the dragoons, were for a short time deprived of speech. Next day, the 25th, we approached Pampeluna; and on this day, the only gun which the French had been able to bring away from Vittoria was taken by Colonel Ross with his horse artillery. In the afternoon we bivouacked at the village of Bancezar, just out of the range of the guns at Pampeluna, where we remained to blockade that fortress.

About the beginning of July Sir Rowland was relieved

from that irksome duty to the more active one of driving General Casan from the fruitful valley of Bastan. On the 3rd we arrived at Iruita. On the 4th and 5th we had severe skirmishing, and drove the enemy from several positions. On the 6th the French moved up, and took possession of the immense mountain to their right, the key of the entrance into the valley. On the morning of the 7th, Sir Rowland, with two British brigades and one Portuguese, ascended the lofty Pyrenees. After a most fatiguing march we reached the top, where we were delighted to find Lord Wellington and his staff, amongst whom we recognised an old friend of the regiment, Colonel May, of the artillery (now Sir John May). Under his Lordship's directions, the enemy were driven from several positions; but in the afternoon a dense fog, so frequent in those lofty regions, coming on, completely put a stop to further operations for that day, it being impossible for the different corps to communicate with each other. We were therefore obliged to remain all night in the different situations in which the fog had caught us. In the course of the night we could plainly hear the French talking under us. His Lordship was on the mountain with us, and shared the fatigues, privations, and anxiety of that memorable night.

The morning of the 28th broke upon us beautifully clear, and shewed the enemy in strong force under us. After a little preparation, we moved down upon them, and in a short time Sir Rowland, with his division, had the honour of first driving the French out of Spain.

After giving them three hearty British cheers, we retired and took possession of the different passes of the Puerte de Maya. The different posts for the picquets having been fixed upon, and the signals of alarm arranged, General Walker's brigade were bivouacked near the main road over the pass; our brigade moved down near the village of Maya, leaving a captain's picquet on the high rock commanding a pass to the right; and having the light companies, under the command of Major Bradbey, half way up the hill as an immediate support, in case of an attack. When on duty on the elevated situation of the rock, we could plainly see the French army in bivouack, near the village of Anhoue.[3]

About the middle of July, the enemy seemed to receive strong re-enforcements, and from the frequent reviews taking place, and the attendance of a numerous staff, it was evident that some person of distinction had joined them;—we soon afterwards found it was Marshal Soult. Major General Pringle having arrived, took command of our brigade.

Everything remained quiet until the afternoon of the 24th, when the French army moved off in strong columns to its left About eleven o'clock in the forenoon of the 25th, two guns from the centre announced to us that the enemy was advancing upon the rock picquet. The brigade instantly fell in and moved up the heights as fast as possible: we soon heard the musketry and saw a murderous conflict going on at the rock. Major Bradbey, on the first alarm, moved rapidly up with the light companies to support the brave picquet of the 34th,—those gallant fellows defending every inch of the post, till they came to the highest pinnacle of the rock, which they retained for some time against fearful numbers. They were almost all killed, wounded, or taken prisoners. Major Bradbey died afterwards of his wounds, at Vittoria.—When we came to the scene of action, we found the 1st brigade, consisting of the 50th, 71st, and 92nd, who had a shorter distance to come than we had, nobly endeavouring to check the terrible dense column of the French, who were advancing under innumerable skirmishers.

The conduct of the 92nd was magnificent; we could

---

3. We were glad to find a great many cherry-trees among the Pyrenees, the delicious fruit of which was a great blessing to us in that sultry weather.

see more of them than the others, and we could not but admire the cool soldier-like manner in which they retired in line for short distances from ten times their numbers, leaving rows of their fine fellows behind them; they were formed to the left of the road leading to the rock. On the 28th coming up, General Pringle instantly formed us in by their side, our left touching their right, and our right being thrown forward, lining a ridge which completely enfiladed the road, up which a French column was advancing to turn the right of the Highlanders. A terrific volley of musketry thrown in by the "Slashers" nearly annihilated the leading regiment, and checked the advance of the remainder—unfortunately a ravine between us prevented the British from charging. The two brigades therefore continued warmly engaged for some time, and the enemy having at length turned us on both flanks, we were obliged to retire from the unequal contest. The 1st brigade, with part of the 2nd, moved along the ridge to the mountain, which we held (the key of the pass) on the night of the seventh; the other part of the 2nd brigade was obliged to retire by Maya and Alisonda[4] On the 26th, we took up a position at Iruita, where we were joined by Sir William Stewart, and that part of the division that obtained possession of the mountain to the left of the valley.

We were sorry to find Sir William wounded in the leg. The coolness displayed by General Pringle, who commanded at the hard fought action of Maya, with two British brigades against two French divisions, was admirable. Early in the action, a fine young man, Ensign Dalmar, of the 28th, while carrying the colours, was shot through the heart by a French sharpshooter. Ensign Hill, seeing the colours fall, instantly

4. At Maya the bravery of some of the French officers was admirable; they often advanced in front of their columns, in face of the 1st brigade, and would plant a flag round which their men would instantly form: several of these fine fellows were knocked over.

ran and took them up, exclaiming at the same time that "the colours of the 'Slashers' should never want a person to display them to the enemy."—He had scarcely spoke, when the same Frenchman, having reloaded, hit him in the same place as poor Dalmar. Fortunately for Hill, he had a handkerchief in his breast, which saved him: the ball passed through his coat, waistcoat, thirteen folds of the handkerchief, and his shirt, giving him a severe contusion in the breast; he suffered from spitting blood for a long time afterwards. This brave fellow died, whilst captain of grenadiers of the 63rd Regiment, in Portugal, in the year 1825. Two or three of our marksmen, having detected the Frenchman picking off our officers, he was soon tumbled down the rocks.

The loss of that excellent officer, Major Bradbey, has already been mentioned.

Captain Mitcham, Lieutenants Tomlinson, Crummer, Gordon, and Ensign Hill, were severely wounded; Captain Irving was wounded, (and taken,) as also were four sergeants, and 147 rank and file. At one time during the action, when the 92nd was retiring beautifully in line, two or three of their fine fellows, who had been wounded in the legs, were seen trying to follow them on their hands and knees. The 34th suffered severely; their gallant commanding officer, Colonel Fenwick, lost a leg, and the captain of grenadiers and Lieutenant Day, were killed.

The conduct of our excellent chaplain, the Reverend Charles Frith, was so truly praiseworthy and humane, that it deserves to be recorded. Being a strong man, he carried down on his back, one after the other, three or four of the officers of our brigade who had been severely wounded, from the heights where the action was fought, to the village of Maya, a distance of a mile and a half. During the whole of the Peninsular campaign, this worthy clergyman was never seen to wear a cloak or great coat

On the afternoon of the 27th, as we were about to retire from Iruita, a person was observed approaching the advanced post in one of our soldier's great coats: one of the picquet called out that it was Sergeant Myers' ghost—and what was our surprise, when we found that it was the man himself! On the 25th he had been pierced through the body by a musket shot, and from loss of blood remained insensible. Just before we retired, he was lifted, still breathing, behind the rock where the body of poor Dalmar was placed, and left by his side to breathe his last—his coat was thrown over him. According to his own story, in the course of the 26th, he awoke as if from a dream, and found nothing but death and desolation around him; he put on his great coat, and with the greatest difficulty, exhausted as he was by loss of blood and hunger, succeeded, by keeping to the mountains, in getting round the strong columns and outposts of the enemy; he fortunately joined us just before we moved off.

The march on the night of the 27th towards Lanz, was a severe one, it being very dark, and the road almost impassable. From the excessive fatigues the men had undergone during the two previous days, they were very drowsy, and ran the risk, every false step they made, of being precipitated over a dreadful precipice to our left. An accident happened to a wagon, drawn by mules belonging to Colonel Ross's troop of horse-artillery, containing his spare shoes and nails, and many valuable stores of that description, which unfortunately fell over, but by the exertions of that officer, with the assistance of some of our men, most of the stores were recovered. The division retired upon Ligasso. The enemy followed us closely on the 28th and 29th, but did not come to action; however we heard hard knocks going on to our right in the neighbourhood of Pampeluna.

On the morning of the 30th, the outlying picquets of

the brigade, under the command of Captain Hartman of the 28th, were attacked by a strong force of the enemy. Captain Hartman gallantly defended his post for seven hours, until turned on both flanks, and when obliged to retire, he covered the retreat of some Portuguese, who were hard pressed, for which he received the thanks of Sir Rowland on his rejoining the brigade. From the ruggedness of the position we occupied, the regiments were all partially engaged; companies and even subdivisions had their turn. In the afternoon, some Portuguese were giving way, on being attacked by a superior force of the enemy, when Captain Hartman, fortunately for him, happened to be near Sir Rowland, with two companies of the 28th. Captain Hartman was ordered to their support, with instructions to rally the Portuguese, and then drive the enemy down the hill; the first instruction was instantly accomplished, and the point of the British bayonet very soon effected the other: on their return, Colonel Rook was sent by Sir Rowland to thank Captain Hartman.

Lieutenant Anderson, of the grenadier company, had collected several small parties of the regiment, who had been separated from their comrades during the engagement, by the abrupt irregularities of the mountain, and was waiting in a narrow road for an opportunity to act; and perceiving the village of El Ariba occupied by the enemy in considerable force, repelling every attempt of a brave detachment of Portuguese to take it, he led his little party of eighteen "Slashers" to their assistance. On his arrival, he found great numbers of the enemy in the streets, far superior to the assailants; but with the coolness and determination for which he was always distinguished, he kept them in check for some time, and finally, with the Portuguese, succeeded in driving the French from the village, and left it in possession of our gallant allies. The conduct of a very powerful fellow, named Tank, of No. 2 company—one of this brave little party—was conspicuous on this occasion. On charging the enemy down the hill towards the village, they came to a precipice, where Tank's muscular arm rendered good service: we could plainly see him from our position, at work with his musket and bayonet, forking the Frenchmen over it like sheaves of corn tossed from a cart On their return, Lieutenant Anderson was thanked by Sir Rowland, and Tank was promoted on the spot. Poor Tank was never heard of after the Battle of Waterloo; he must have fallen unperceived: he was regretted as a gallant soldier.

The enemy having now threatened our left, the division was withdrawn by Sir Rowland in a masterly manner to a ridge in the rear, without suffering any material loss. When we remained for the night under shelter of our cloaks, tired and fatigued, and scarcely thinking of what was to be done on the morrow, we found Sir Rowland had lain within a few paces of the centre of the 28th.

The morning of the 31st broke with unusual splendour on the lofty Pyrenees. On standing to our arms, the officers and men were thanked for their conduct on the preceding day. We were glad to find that the enemy had retired, having been defeated in every attempt to throw supplies into Pampeluna.

Sir Rowland's corps pursued the enemy by the road to the pass of Donna Maria; and on our arrival at the foot of the hill, we came up with them, ascending in great haste. The men were overjoyed on finding Sir William Stewart on his favourite charger, again at the,head of the division; the wound he received on the 25th was still open, but he could not be restrained, and had a pillow placed between his leg and the saddle. The enemy having taken up a strong position in great force, the 7th division, under the Earl of Dalhousie, moved to the attack by a road to the right, parallel to that which we occupied. Sir William Stewart advanced with the first brigade, and drove in their numerous skirmishers, when he was again unfortunately wounded by a shot through the arm. On passing us to the rear, we expressed our regret; but he replied, "My gallant friends, it is only the fortune of war." The command now devolved upon General Pringle, and of the brigade on Colonel O'Callaghan. The several regiments were now ordered to advance, and in a very short time, assisted by the 7th division, and giving them three cheers, we drove the French at the point of the bayonet, from their strong position at the pass. The enemy suffered severely: we pursued them some distance down the other side; but a thick fog coming on, or rather a cloud that had descended from the mountain top, obliged us to give up the chase. The storming of the pass of Donna Maria, was the last of our share of the ever-memorable battles of the Pyrenees. In the afternoon, we moved to and bivouacked at Almandos; and on the two last days we were very fortunate, having only had one killed, and three wounded.

On the 1st of August, we advanced by the pass of Lannes, and on the 4th, we again took up the position in which we had fought on the 25th, proudly looking down on our discomfited foes;—as soon as the regiment was dismissed, several of us visited the spot where poor Dalmar was laid; we found a week's sun had made a sad alteration in him, his pockets had been searched, and by his side was part of a most affectionate letter from his sister, which brought tears into many eyes. We consigned his remains to as deep a grave as the rocky mountain side would permit It was melancholy to see the number of dead lying in every direction, and so disagreeable was the stench, that we were obliged next day to change our ground: we likewise sought the place where our regiment caused such destruction to the column that was advancing by the road, to turn the 92nd. Great was our surprise when we found it was the French 28th Regiment, which had been so severely handled by us! A few days after the action, Major Irving, who was taken prisoner, saw the skeleton of the regiment, consisting of two officers, four non-commissioned officers, and a few men pass through Bayonne, on their way to the depot to fill up. We remained in the neighbourhood of Maya, until the 10th, when Sir Rowland's corps moved to the right; we bivouacked on the night of the 10th at Los Aldudes, and on the 11th, took up our ground on the heights of the celebrated Ronces-Valles; strong working parties were employed constructing block-houses to defend the different passes. We changed ground frequently; the different regiments taking their turn of the advanced posts for a week at a time.

The 15th of August, being Napoleon's birthday, reports were in circulation that Soult would make another attempt, which kept us all on the alert. On the 23rd, it being our turn to have a little rest, we descended from the heights, and encamped at the village of Burguetta, below Ronces-Valles. About this time we were joined by the following officers— Captain Kelly, Captain Farr, Lieutenants Kelly, Carruthers, Shelton, Clarke, and Dears, with a detachment of men.

While we were resting from our toils, some of the officers requested Colonel Belson to send a party to Pasages, near St Sebastian, (where supplies of every description were brought from England for the army), and to purchase tobacco for the men, and tea and sugar for the officers: 2,000 dollars were collected, and given in charge to Sergeant Ball[5] and six grenadiers. The conduct of these brave fellows on this occasion was chivalrous in the extreme—

5. This fine fellow, on a former occasion, received a musket ball through the fleshy part of his leg, when he very quietly took the quid out of his mouth, applied it to the wound, tied it up, and thought no more of the matter.

proving beyond all doubt, that British soldiers possess a high sense of honour and heroism, and that they are not, as supposed by many, mere machines.—The party arrived at Pasages on the 30th, and learning that St. Sebastian was to be stormed the next day, the sergeant addressed his men, telling them there was hardly an action in the Peninsula in which the 28th had not a share, and proposed to them to volunteer on the storming party, for the credit of their regiment. To this the men joyfully assented, and the next question was, how to dispose of the money safely, with which they had been entrusted. It was determined to place it in the hands of a commissary, taking his receipt for the amount, which document the sergeant again lodged in the hands of a third person.

Having thus carefully provided for the property of their officers, those brave fellows volunteered for the desperate enterprise, and joined the ranks of their gallant comrades of Barossa heights—the grenadiers of the 9th. It would be superfluous to say, they did their duty, and most fortunately—indeed singularly—none of them were hurt. After the town was taken, the gallant sergeant collected his men, reclaimed the money, purchased the supplies, and returned to his regiment with a handsome testimonial of their conduct, addressed to Colonel Belson, from the general commanding the brigade.

Whilst we were encamped near Ronces Valles, an old Irish soldier of the grenadiers, met Sir William Stewart, on his way to rejoin, on recovering from the wound he had received at the pass of Donna Maria, and addressed him thus: "God bless your honour, I am glad to see you again."

The general, with his usual kindness, asked how his old friends of the 28th were, to which the answer was, "They were quite well, but they had not had a drop of *extra* since he left them;" as soon as the general had passed, the old hand, taking a near road to the camp, made known that Sir William was coming. The report ran like wildfire; so that by the time he arrived, every one was out to receive him with three cheers; Paddy's hint had also the desired effect; for soon after, the welcome call was heard through the camp, "A man of a mess for rum." Sir William was a great favourite with the men; for whenever the weather was wet, or they had undergone great fatigue, he gave them an extra allowance.

After changing our position several times, we relieved a Portuguese brigade on the heights of Aldudes. We were here badly off for forage for our animals, and were obliged to send strong foraging parties down into Navarre, which brought on some sharp skirmishing with the natives. We were now perched on one of the highest of the lower Pyrenees, envying our more fortunate enemies in their snug huts in the fertile plains of Navarre. The Portuguese had left us excellent huts, which we took choice of according to rank. We were almost isolated; our principal amusement consisted in loosening immense rocks from the top of the mountain, and letting them roll down the French side; the noise was appalling, and trees of large size gave way before them. About the end of October, a fire broke out among the huts occupied by some poor women and children; many of them were burnt out; and what added to their distress, the rigours of a Pyrenean winter had just set in. Colonel Belson lost his excellent hut in a similar way, and with difficulty saved his baggage.

Towards the beginning of November, the snow began to fall very heavily. On the 2nd we nearly lost two valuable officers, Lieutenants Irwin and Carruthers, of the grenadiers, in the following manner, A company of the regiment fell in every morning before daylight, and moved up the pass, where they remained until an hour after sunrise, in case of an attack. On that morning, it fortunately happened to be the turn of my company—the grenadiers. On arriving at the parade, I missed my officers; on which I immediately went to their tent, calling several times, but receiving no answer: somewhat surprised, I cut the cords, and threw the door open, when to my astonishment, I found Lieutenant Irwin hardly able to crawl out, and Lieutenant Carruthers lying in a state of insensibility. He was instantly carried out, and both in a short time, with medical assistance, recovered. It appeared that they had very improperly, the night before, retired to rest with some charcoal embers in their tent; a snow-storm coming on, had filled up every crevice; and if their company had not been for duty that morning, it is most probable they would have perished.

The storms becoming very,severe, we were moved down, and put into the village of Los Aldudes, leaving Captain Gale with a company on the mountains: this was the first time for six months that either officers or men had their heads under a roof.[6]

On the 6th, Captain Gale was recalled; and on the 8th we moved to Maya, and encamped on the old ground which we occupied previous to the battle of the 25th of July. We were now aware that a descent was about to be made into France, which put us all into high spirits.

On the afternoon of the 9th, we were joined by a detachment from England, under Captain Carroll, of one lieutenant, one ensign, one sergeant, and thirty-three rank and file; and in about an hour afterwards the corps of Sir Rowland

---

6. During the war, we had often been halted in ploughed fields, with no comfort near us—not a bush or a tree to shelter us,—we generally passed the night in the following manner: two of us would sit down upon a stone, with our cloaks rolled about us, back to back, supporting each other, our feet like-wife upon stones, to keep them out of the wet. It is an old soldier's maxim upon service, "Sleep when you can; you can always eat, if you have any thing to eat."

moved up to the top of the Maya Pass, where we remained under arms until the rising of the moon, which was to be the signal for the different columns to move down into France. At ten, the long-wished for moon rose with more than usual brightness and by her light we marched with joyful steps down the rugged sides of this wonderful barrier, when we bade farewell to the Peninsula, the scene of so many hard-fought actions, and where we had left so many of our gallant comrades.

## CHAPTER 8

# Nivelle, Nive and St. Pierre

1813. On the morning of the 10th November, when we descended into the French territory, we remained under arms till day-light, when a cannonade from the centre announced the signal for the British columns to advance to attack the enemy in the strong position which he had been for three months fortifying. Sir Rowland had the command of the right; Sir William Stewart commanded the second division.

It was an imposing spectacle. As far as the eye could reach, the masses of red jackets were seen moving to the points of the French lines in their immediate front The cold and privation of the preceding night were entirely forgotten. Our brigade, under Major-General Pringle, having driven in the enemy's outposts on the Nivelle and in front of Anhoue, were supplied with scaling-ladders, and ordered to move to the left, and storm a strong redoubt on the centre of their position. We were then under a heavy fire of shot and shell from the enemy's line of forts. Just as we had crowned a height on the left of the river, and were in the act of descending to cross and storm, we saw the Sixth Division, under General Lambert, which had already advanced to the left of our hill, had already crossed, and were moving up towards the redoubt. Their conduct was truly gallant; taking the fort did not cause them the least check. We moved up their right, and bringing up our left shoulders, assisted the gallant Highlanders to clear the remainder of the position. Major-General Byng, with the 3rd brigade, having carried the entrenchments, and a redoubt on the enemy's left, in which they suffered severely, brought their bivouac, in rear of the position, entirely in our possession, the enemy flying in the direction of Bayonne.

The enemy's bivouack was the most complete we had ever seen, the huts were so admirably constructed, and the streets and squares so uniform. It had been well supplied with shops and canteens, but everything useful had been destroyed; we found nothing but empty casks and bottles. Many of the huts had been set on fire, in which were a number of muskets, probably belonging to wounded men, who had been carried to the rear: many of them being loaded, went off occasionally, to the danger of the captors, long after the enemy were out of sight In the afternoon we advanced a short distance, and bivouacked for the night. In this brilliant affair the second division suffered a severe loss in their Adjutant-General, Colonel Rooke, who was mortally wounded at the top of the position. His conduct and address had endeared him to everyone.

In the battle of the Nivelle our regiment had only a few men wounded. When the brigade was advancing to storm the fort, which was taken by the Sixth Division, a regiment of Sir John Hamilton's Portuguese was a little in advance of us to our left, moving in column of sections of five file, when a shell fell into one of them, killed nine, and broke the right arm of a tenth man, who, as we passed, was upon his knees, crossing himself with his left hand, and thanking his Maker that it was no worse with him. I may be pardoned here for relating an anecdote of an old comrade of our's. Captain Blakeney, of the 36th regiment, (who, it may be remembered, obtained his company, when a lieutenant in the 28th, for his conduct at Arroyo del Molino,) was one of the Sixth Division, and on advancing up the hill to attack the fort, his left leg was fractured by a grape shot. Two of his men offered to take him to the rear;—"No," said he, "when the fort is taken, I will be much obliged to you for your assistance." During this interval, he stood upon his right leg, holding by a tree, waving his cap in the other hand to cheer his men. Of course he very soon obtained assistance, and was carried to the village of Anhone in a blanket.

Lieutenant Irwin, of the 28th Grenadiers, when on duty with the baggage guard, had an unexpected opportunity of distinguishing himself. A considerable force of the enemy, who had advanced towards our extreme right, by the narrow pass at the rock picquet, came down, and attacked the baggage at Maya. Lieutenant Irwin was the first officer on the spot, where, with a few servants and bat-men, he kept them at bay, until the convalescents who were in the village got under arms. The French, seeing a strong force preparing to receive them, retired, closely and bravely pursued by Lieutenant Irwin, who, with his handful of men, drove them back over the mountain. Before the French were checked, they had succeeded in plundering some baggage belonging to the cavalry; and the pay-master of the 13th Dragoons lost a large sum in guineas.

On the 12th the brigade advanced, and took up a position on the banks of the Nive, between Cambo and the ford of Elsa, where there was a mill occupied by the enemy. A party of the 34th advanced to reconnoitre it, when the French opened a heavy fire, and knocked down the serjeant-major and two men. The party was obliged to retire. A few minutes afterwards, the enemy generously allowed a few men to go out and carry in their wounded comrades. Next day we retired, and encamped near Espaletta the weather becoming very severe; and on the 18th we went into cantonments in the village of La Rosoir, situated on a narrow curve of the Nive. In consequence of the severe weather, the river was a complete barrier between the two armies. The French had a sentry on the opposite bank, within half musket-shot, absolutely looking into our windows. The French, as well as ourselves, were much tired with the toils and fatigues of the past; so that we enjoyed ourselves very much in our miserable houses, and never molested each other. This was the first time we were in a French village. The people did not know what to make of us at first; but from the judicious proclamations of the commander-in-chief, recommending them to remain in their houses, and assuring them that everything would be paid for, they soon gained confidence. The poultry of France, of which we had heard so much, but of which we had yet seen nothing, began to make its appearance, and to our astonishment, we found it was kept in the garrets of the houses. Markets were now established, and those that had money could get luxuries to which they had long been strangers and those that could get none, were contented with soup and *bouillé* one day, and *bouillé* and soup the other. While in cantonments, Brevet Lieutenant-Colonel Ross relieved Brevet Lieutenant-Colonel Nixon, who went home to take the command of the second battalion. On Colonel Ross being shown to his house, which overhung the narrow curve of the river, he was not a little surprised to see a French sentry within pistol-shot of him. It was the first he had seen since his return from England.

The French officers and ours soon became intimate; we used to meet at a narrow part of the river, and talk over the campaign. They would never believe (or pretended not to believe) the reverse of Napoleon in Germany: and when we received the news of the Orange Boven affair in Holland, they said that it was impossible to convince them. One of our officers took the *Star* newspaper, rolled a stone upon it, and attempted to throw it across the river; unfortunately the stone went through it, and it fell into the water. The French officer very quietly said in tolerably good English "your good news is very soon damped."

While we were in cantonments, Lieutenant Irwin, having been with Assistant Surgeon Lavans, to visit some of the 6th Division at Ustaritz, a little way down the river to our left, had a little adventure on their return. A French sentry, perhaps thinking they had left the road, fired towards them from a considerable distance: the ball passed over their heads but happened to kill a plover. Lieutenant Irwin rode up to where the bird dropped, dismounted, picked it up, and making a low bow to the Frenchman rode off. The weather being remarkably fine at the end of November and beginning of December, and the Nive being lower and the roads passable, preparations were made on the afternoon of the 8th December, for an advance.

Lieutenant-Colonel Ross's troops of horse artillery arrived to cover the passage of the river, next morning, the 28th Regiment being ordered to lead with the light companies. The brigade was formed an hour before daylight, by the side of a convent, opposite the ford. Lieutenant-Colonel Ross's guns were placed on a height to our left, with orders to open a cannonade on the mill the moment he could, which was to be the signal for our attack. We had not waited long when Ross's guns sounded the advance; the light companies dashed down to the banks, and opened a heavy fire upon the enemy,—the regiment moving down rapidly though steadily, to the ford. The first thing we saw was the body of Sergeant Bangher, of our light company, lying at the brink, shot through the head, his head lying in the water. We were in sections, and the men as quickly as possible put their pouches on their heads, entered the river, firmly linked together by their arms, and in this manner the "Slashers," in the face of a galling fire, stemmed the mountain torrent, and gained the opposite bank. We found we had still the mill-dam to cross, which was about half as broad, but deeper than the river—it was passed in the same manner. We instantly pushed up the hill as fast as our wet clothes would permit us, and at the point of the bayonet drove the enemy out of Elsa, which we kept till the 34th and 39th, who gallantly supported us, joined. General Pringle expressed himself much pleased with the regiment on this occasion.

Captain Taylor had his left thigh shattered, between the river and the dam, by a musket ball, and several of our poor fellows, who were wounded, were taken down by the current and drowned.

I recollect that on the evening previous to crossing the Nive, Paymaster Dewes, of our regiment, gave a supper party to a few officers. We were all aware of the hazardous nature of the enterprise before us; but soldier-like, prone to the enjoyment of the present, and careless of the future, we spent a most joyous and happy evening. About midnight, Colonel Ross, whose guns were to cover the passage of the river, rose and said, "Gentlemen, we have spent a delightful evening together; 'tis now time we should part, to prepare ourselves for the struggle which awaits us. Let us fill a bumper, and drink success to our arms, and that we may all be as comfortable tomorrow night as we now are."— Having done so, we all shook hands and departed: in less than two hours after, the thunder of Ross's guns announced that the bloody strife had begun.

The enemy, having been forced back by the 1st brigade, at Cambo,—higher up the river, to our right,—we waited some time for them, and likewise for the passage of General

Buchan's brigade of Portuguese, who were not so fortunate as we were, they having had several men drowned in crossing. The enemy, beaten back in every direction, retired upon Bayonne. We advanced, and had some smart skirmishing in the afternoon,—No. 6, 7, 8, and light company, being warmly engaged till the day closed, leaving the French in position on the heights of St. Pierre. In this action we had one sergeant, one drummer, and six men killed, one captain, two sergeants, one drummer, and thirty-five wounded. The enemy threw a number of shells at us, but fortunately without effect. In the course of the day, our left touched the gallant light companies of the 6th division, who had crossed below at Ustaritz; they, with the 8th Portuguese, under Colonel Douglas, and the 9th Caçadores, under Colonel Browne, drove the enemy from Ville Franche. The light company of the 42nd, suffered a severe loss in Captain Stewart, and Lieutenant Stewart, who were both killed: they were buried in one grave. The feelings expressed by the men at the fate of their officers is indescribable, and did equal honour to the living and the slain.

The afternoon and night of the 9th was extremely wet; the rain fell in torrents; and we had no covering whatever but our cloaks: we crouched around our fires, with our feet as close to them as possible.

On the morning of the 10th, when we arose from our cold and hard couches, we found the French had retired from St Pierre. Sir Rowland advanced, and with his corps took up that position (resting his right upon the Adour, and his left upon the Nive, at Ville Franche, where the 28th were), which was three days afterwards to display to his country his judgement, and the gallantry of the troops he commanded.

On the tenth, eleventh, and twelfth, there was severe fighting on the left of the army; and from our position we could plainly see the different attacks made by the enemy, and were delighted to see them as often bravely repulsed.

Soult, not being able to make any impression upon our gallant comrades on the left, on the afternoon of the twelfth withdrew a great part of his army into Bayonne, with the intention of trying his success with Sir Rowland. We guessed what he was about, and were ready to receive him.

## Battle of St. Pierre

At daybreak on the morning of the 13th December, Marshal Soult attacked the right of the British army, with a force of 30,000 men, when a most bloody action commenced, and continued till about three in the afternoon, when the enemy were beaten back in every direction, with an immense loss of men, and two guns. The gallantry of the regiment and picquet was most conspicuous. The outposts on the first attack at daybreak were reinforced by the inlying picquets under my command; and during the whole day we were engaged with a much superior force in front of Ville Franche, and finally drove them back. The men fired from 160 to 170 rounds each. We suffered much on this hard fought day, having Captain Wolfe, Lieutenants Clarke, Nelson, Keep, and Ensign Waring, wounded severely; six rank and file killed, four sergeants, one drummer, and eighty-six wounded. We were relieved by a brigade of the 3d division; when we retired to the rear of St Pierre, where we lay upon our arms that night.

The hero of the Peninsula having arrived on the ground, just as the battle was over, rode up to Sir Rowland, and shaking him by the hand, is reported to have said "Hill! this glorious day is all your own."

It is but justice to say that the Portuguese brigade, under General Buchan, and Colonel Ashworth, behaved admirably. Sir Rowland, with his corps of 10,000, did their day's work gallantly, having heartily thrashed the first Marshal of France, at the head of 30,000. The French acknowledged to have lost 8,000; but from the appearance of the field, many more must have fallen. The carnage made by the guns of that gallant officer, Colonel Ross, of the royal artillery, upon the enemy's columns, was tremendous,—the dead were actually lying in heaps.

On the morning of the fourteenth, the division was moved up to St. Pierre, and formed near the main road. Colonel Belson was thanked by Sir William Stewart and General Pringle, for the gallantry of the regiment, and Colonel Ross and myself for the conduct of the picquets. The scene of slaughter along the road towards Bayonne, was frightful; the road was so covered with dead, that it was impossible to ride over it. This was their principal point of attack; it was bravely defended by the 1st brigade under General Barnes. The 92nd suffered more than any regiment in this division, and their gallant conduct was most conspicuous.

A singular instance of presentiment occurred on this occasion. When the inlying picquets turned out in the morning, a soldier of my company, the grenadiers, named M'Kinlay, came up to me handing a paper, and said, "Captain, here is my will; I am to be killed today, and I will all my arrears, and everything I have, to my comrade Hugh Swift"

"What nonsense, M'Kinlay," I replied to him; "go into action, and do what you have always done, behave like a brave soldier."

He answered, "I will do that, Sir; but I am certain I am to be killed today, and I request you to take my will."

To satisfy him I took it, and the man fought with the picquets during the whole day with great coolness and gallantry. In the afternoon, a little before the action was over, we rejoined the regiment,—we had suffered much, but

M'Kinlay was standing unhurt close to me; upon which I observed to him, "So, M'Kinlay, I suspect you are wrong this time."

The right of the regiment being posted on the round end of a hill cut into steps for the vines, a body of the enemy's sharpshooters came close under us, and opened a fire to cover their retiring columns. M'Kinlay, seeing one of them taking aim over the arm of a fig-tree in our direction, exclaimed, "Look at that rascal going to shoot our captain!" And advancing one step down the hill, presented at the Frenchman, who, however, was unfortunately too quick for him, for in an instant afterwards poor M'Kinlay was shot through the neck, and killed on the spot. The same ball gave me a severe contusion on the breast, and I fell with the unfortunate man, and was actually covered with his blood. He was one of the best soldiers in the grenadier company, and was much regretted;—indeed but for him it is probable I should not have lived to tell this tale. The will was duly forwarded to the War-office, whence an order was issued for his comrade Swift to receive all that was due to him[1].

During a few days after the action, our brigade was quartered in farm houses, in the neighbourhood of St. Pierre, whence we went into cantonments in the village of Pitte Maguire, called by the soldiers Pat M'Guire.

The day after the action, several of the officers went to the barrier, where we saw some of our brave enemies with whom we had become acquainted at the Nive. We shewed to each other the escapes we had had, by the balls tearing our clothes, and going through our caps: several of them observed, "that they had been in many actions with Napoleon

1. An excellent letter was written by Lieutenant French, of the 23rd Fusiliers (now major of the 28th,) then composing part of the 4th division, who were looking on from a height, ready to assist us in case of need, to the father of one of our wounded officers, expressing their admiration of the bravery of the regiment.

in Germany, but they had never seen such hard fighting as they had since they had been opposed to the British."

We were now two miles in the rear, but took our turn with the 34th and 39th in coming up to the alarm post an hour before daybreak. Lieutenant Nelson, of our regiment, who was shot through the body on the 13th, was able, by means of his high spirits, and an excellent constitution, to go out snipe-shooting, about the third or fourth day after.

## Chapter 9
# Orthes & Toulouse

1814. January set in with dreadful weather; but though we were in the most miserable houses, we made ourselves comfortable and happy; and we had now and then an opportunity of getting luxuries from St Jean de Luz, such as Irish potatoes and butter. We now took our turn of the picquets at the barrier about half-way between St. Pierre and Bayonne, with the Highland brigade of the sixth division, which we did by companies. About the middle of January, when the grenadiers—28th—were on this duty, a daring fellow, an Irishman, named Tom Patten, performed a singular feat. At the barrier there was a rivulet, along which our line of sentries was posted. To the right was a thick low wood, and during the cessation of hostilities, our officers had again become intimate with those of the French, and the soldiers had actually established a traffic in tobacco and brandy, in the following ingenious manner. A large stone was placed in that part of the rivulet screened by the wood, opposite to a French sentry, on which our people used to put a canteen with a quarter-dollar, for which it was very soon filled with brandy.

One afternoon, about dusk, Patten had put down his canteen, with the usual money in it, and retired; but though he returned several times, no canteen was there. He waited till the moon rose, but still he found nothing on the stone. When it was near morning, Tom thought he saw the same sentry there who was there when he put his canteen down; so he sprang across the stream, seized the unfortunate Frenchman, wrested his firelock from him, and actually shaking him out of his accoutrements, recrossed, vowing he would keep them until he got his canteen of brandy, and brought them to the picquet-house. Two or three hours afterwards, just as we were about to fall in, an hour before daybreak, the serjeant came to say that a flag of truce was at the barrier. I instantly went down, when I found the officer of the French picquet, in a state of great alarm, saying that a most extraordinary circumstance had occurred, (relating the adventure,) and stating, that if the sentry's arms and accoutrements were not given back, his own commission would be forfeited, as well as the life of the poor sentry. A sergeant was instantly sent to see if they were in the picquet-house, when Patten came up, scratching his head, saying, "he had them in pawn for a canteen of brandy and a quarter-dollar," and told us the story in his way, whereupon the things were immediately given over to the French captain, who stepping behind, put two five-*franc* pieces into Patten's hand. Tom, however, was not to be bribed by an enemy; but generously handed the money to his officer, requesting that he would insist on the French captain taking the money back.

The Frenchman was delighted to get the firelock and accoutrements back; and the joy of the poor fellow who was stripped of them may be conceived, as, if it had been reported, he would certainly have been shot by sentence of court-martial in less than forty-eight hours. Patten, however, was confined, and reported to Sir Rowland, and in a few days after he was tried, and sentenced by a court-martial to receive 300 lashes. The British regiments of the division were collected at the alarm-post, when Tom was brought out, and his sentence read, and Sir Rowland, in an excellent speech, addressed the man and regiments assembled, on the unprecedented crime of which he had been guilty, justly observing, that the consequences of his imprudence might have cost the lives of thousands; but the general, being informed of his gallantry on many occasions from the passage of the Douro, and Talavera, was pleased to remit the sentence, to the great delight of every one present Paddy on his return to his quarters got three cheers from the company for his good fortune.

On the 8th February, we left our winter-quarters, in which, miserable as they were, we spent some pleasant nights, and moved to St. Pierre, and on the 12th, to the village of Yatsa. Here Colonel Belson being taken dangerously ill, was obliged to be left behind. Colonel Ross succeeded to the regiment and Major Mullins, having the command of the light companies, I became acting major.

On the 14th[1] we advanced, and came upon the enemy's picquets on the Joyeuse. The French, under General Harispe, in position at Hellete, were gallantly attacked by the first and and third brigades, under Generals Barnes and Byng, and driven back with loss.

On the 15th we continued the pursuit; and after a long march, about an hour before sunset, we heard skirmishing in front, the sound of which always makes the men as fresh as when they started. We found it proceeded from the Spaniards driving the enemy's out-posts, they having taken up a strong position in front of Garris, and had been reinforced by a division under General Paris.

We arrived at the foot of the hill, about half an hour be-

1. This day that brave officer, Major Cameron, of the Buffs, was severely wounded in the mouth. He behaved most gallantly on the 13th of December, in driving with his light company a very superior force from the town of Vieux Maguire.

fore dusk, when Sir Rowland gave orders for an immediate attack. The British brigades, under Sir William Stewart, moved up the hill in the most gallant manner, and notwithstanding the strength of the position, drove them in every direction. They made several desperate attempts to regain it, but were always repulsed, particularly twice, when they were bravely received, and driven back by the 39th, under the Hon. Colonel O'Callaghan. His horse was shot, and he was leading his regiment on foot, when he was attacked by three French officers. The gallant colonel, being an old dragoon, was an excellent swordsman, and a fine powerful fellow. He cut down one at the first blow, and taking his sword in his left hand, attacked the other two. By a back blow he houghed the second, and then the third was an easy victory. The action continued until after dark. Our brigade suffered a severe loss in its gallant leader, General Pringle, who was shot through the body. In this brisk affair we had one rank and file killed; Captain Gale, Lieutenant Gordon, and six rank and file, wounded; Captain Gale died of his wounds next day.

In the action of Garris there were ten officers and 200 of the French taken prisoners, who belonged to the Catalonian army, and had not been accustomed to such a handling. A shocking imposition was practised upon two of our officers, Lieutenants I—— and C——, that evening. Some time after the action, a Portuguese soldier came to their tent with some pork-steaks to dispose of, which their servants eagerly purchased, and dressed them for their masters' supper. They being very tired and hungry after a long march and hard fighting, sat down and made a hearty meal: but a short time after, what was their surprise and disgust, when they discovered it to be more than equivocal that the alleged "pork-steaks" had not long before belonged to the person of a Frenchman! I——, like an old soldier, drank off half a tumbler of brandy, and thought no more of the matter; but poor C—— turned very sick, and was always ill whenever the subject of their cannibal repast was mentioned.

The enemy retired across the river at St Palais, and destroyed the bridge; but by the activity of our engineers it was soon repaired, and we crossed next day.

On the 17th the enemy were driven across the Gave de Mouleon. They attempted in vain to destroy the bridge at Arriveneto. A most brilliant exploit was here performed by the 92nd Highlanders, in presence of our division. There were two battalions of French strongly posted in the village. A ford was discovered above the bridge, through which Colonel Cameron gallantly led his regiment, under cover of Captain Bean's horse artillery, and drove the enemy out of the village with considerable loss. The French retired upon Sauveterre. The guns were so well served, that many of the enemy were knocked down as they crossed a field in their retreat. In consequence of the gallantry displayed by the 92nd here and at Maya, the names of the two places were inserted in the family arms of their gallant chief; and the Prince Regent gave him as supporters two of the regiment in full costume. For some days we were cantoned in such miserable farm-houses, that, cold as the weather was, several of us were obliged to pitch our tents outside.

On the 24th, the division crossed the Gave d'Oleron at Villeneuve. The enemy evacuated Sauveterre, blowing up the bridge, and retired upon Orthes. We followed, and arrived on the 26th on the heights opposite the town. The French, under the Duke of Dalmatia, were strongly posted behind the town, and the bridge over the Gave de Pau was strongly barricaded.

The left and centre of the army having crossed below the town on the morning of the 27th, they attacked the enemy's position, when a most obstinate action took place. During its progress, Sir Rowland moved up the left bank, and forced the passage of the Gave at a ford some distance above the town, the first and third brigades suffering a slight loss. The corps of Sir Rowland being now on the left and rear of the French—their right being beaten—they began to retire in excellent order; but we, by our rapid movement, having gained the main road to St. Sever, their retreat soon turned into a perfect flight; and as they turned off the road, the 7th Hussars had an opportunity of distinguishing themselves, and making many prisoners. The second division moved along the road parallel to the enemy, who soon began to throw away their arms and packs, and got away. A little before dusk we gave up the pursuit, and bivouacked for the night in some vineyards, where we should have suffered much from the cold, if the complete rout of the French army had not enabled us to collect a great many muskets, the butts of which made excellent fires. The bridge leading to the town was forced by General Buchan with his Portuguese.

On the 28th, the second division moved upon Aire; but the rain now falling in torrents, we were halted. Our brigade, under the Hon. Colonel O'Callaghan, took possession of a small village on the left bank of the Adour, a day's march from Aire, where the enemy had two divisions strongly posted, defending a magazine.

On the 2nd of March, Sir Rowland attacked with the first and third brigades, under Sir William Stewart and La Costa's Portuguese: after a severe contest, he drove them from their position and the town. We missed this brilliant affair, owing to the dragoon who was sent for us losing his way. We did not come up till the next day. The second division was unfortunate in again losing their Adjutant-General, Colonel Hood, whose funeral was attended by all the officers. We were quartered in Aire till the 10th, when we moved forward, and occupied some miserable farm-houses.

On the 16th we advanced to the small village of Servin, where we remained on the 17th. On the 18th we again advanced, and came up with the enemy, strongly posted in the village of Lembige. Partial skirmishing had been going on for several days past, and it was now the turn of the 28th; we were ordered to attack and drive the enemy from the village. The regiment advanced, under cover of Colonel Ross's horse artillery, which had gallantly pushed up to assist us, and opened a destructive cannonade on the village. After a severe contest, in which the light company suffered much, the right wing, under my command, drove them in every direction, and gained possession of the village. In the evening, a little before dusk, just after the outposts had been planted, the French made a desperate attack in great force, but were very soon repulsed, when we remained quiet for the night.

In this affair, Sir William Stewart was pleased with the conduct of the regiment, and I had the honour to receive his thanks for the behaviour of my gallant companions, and was in consequence recommended for promotion. We suffered severely: Lieutenant Gordon, an excellent officer of the light company, and one sergeant, and six rank and file, were killed. Captain Carroll, Lieutenant Gilbert, and thirty rank and file wounded, three rank and file missing. A sad fate attended poor Carroll; he was wounded in the shoulder, and the ball having unfortunately carried into the flesh a part of the bullion of his wing, it caused a locked jaw. He died at Aire a few days afterwards. Never was a brother officer more justly and deeply regretted.

Our captains of light infantry were unfortunate, though certainly they had been much exposed in skirmishing. Poor

Carroll was the third that had fallen within a very short time; still the command of the company was eagerly taken by Captain (now Major) Briggs, of Strathairly, who gallantly led it through the remainder of the campaign, until he was promoted. After the enemy had been driven back in the evening, a cottage was discovered to be on fire, near to which a picquet was posted, under the command of Lieutenant Irwin; it had been ransacked by the French. Lieutenant Irwin heard the groans of a person in the midst of the smoke; he instantly proposed to go in, and endeavour to save him, but as we had no rope to pull him back, in case he should fail from suffocation, we clasped each other by the hands; in this manner Irwin went in, and feeling about for a short time, got hold of and dragged out a poor old man, who was unable to save himself; he was almost in a state of suffocation. On his recovery, he was not a little astonished to find his life had been saved by British officers.

On the 19th, we continued the pursuit; and on the 20th, Sir Rowland, with his corps, marched into Tarbes, driving in their advanced posts, when we halted for a short time. The enemy was in position on strong heights on the other side of the river, while we were halted in Tarbes. That fine brigade, Bock's heavy Germans, passed through to the front. The men having gold lace on their coats, and wearing cocked hats, and their horses being in high condition, the surprised natives asked us if they were not *all officers.* We found an excellent hotel there; the first we had seen since we entered France. Sir R. Hill having made his arrangements, the division crossed the Adour, and formed columns for the attack; but the enemy did not wait to receive us—they retired in all directions, contented with throwing a few long shots at us. The French now retreated rapidly in the direction of Toulouse.

On the 22nd, our advance guard of cavalry, under the

command of General Fane, came up with their rear at St Gaudens. The 13th Dragoons were ordered to attack. Their gallant chief, Colonel Dogherty, calling his two sons[2],—the one a captain, the other a lieutenant,—he placed the eldest (Pat) on his right, and the youngest (George) on his left, and with Major Dunbar, B.M., led the charge. This gallant corps in a very short time, cut the 10th French Hussars to pieces, taking upwards of 100 men and horses. Captain MacAlister, who commanded the advance, distinguished himself. When we came up, the sight was truly melancholy! Throughout the many actions in which we had taken share, we never had seen men and horses so dreadfully mangled: the horses were sold next day; but the best brought very little. The enemy continued their retreat, and we arrived in front of Toulouse in the beginning of April, when we were put in the most delightful villas. The pontoon bridge being laid over the Garonne, above the town, Sir Rowland's corps crossed; but the roads were so bad, that we returned and took up our comfortable cantonments again, the other divisions of the army having crossed by the pontoons, thrown over some distance below the town. On the evening of the 9th, some forward movements of our cavalry indicated that something was to be done next day.

## Battle of Toulouse

At daybreak on the morning of the 10th of April (Easter Sunday), we could plainly see, with our glasses, the British columns moving round to the enemy's right; and at the same time, the 3rd and Light Divisions moved up the right bank, opposite to the spot where we were posted, and commenced the action. About eight a. m., the 28th moved

---

1. The eldest of those two fine young men died in India; the life of the other was saved by his watch at Waterloo,—he is a major in the 27th.

down to the bank of the river, and drove in some of the enemy's outposts, with which we were warmly engaged for some time.

The French having fortified a large mill in the suburbs of St. Cyprien, which annoyed us much, about two p. m., Sir Rowland ordered the 28th to attack it. It was carried in good style by the right wing, in about ten minutes, taking an officer and some prisoners; many made their escape when they saw us advancing with such determination. We suffered considerably; but our loss would have been greater, had it not been for the cool and determined conduct of Lieutenant Irwin, of the grenadiers. As we were advancing on the mill, our men falling very fast, he perceived that the enemy had a dry brick wall about ten feet high, loop-holed, from which they kept up a heavy fire: he ran forward, and leaping a ditch in front of it, sprang at the wall, got hold of the top with his hands, and tugged until he brought a large piece of it down. The grenadiers soon made a gap in it, when we rushed through, and instantly took the place. The French were soon afterwards driven by the division from the whole of the suburbs to the shelter of the old walls of the town, where we kept them. Sir Rowland and Sir William Stewart were much pleased with the conduct of the 28th, and sent Colonel Curry to thank them.

The enemy now brought two guns to the bridge on the canal, nearly opposite to us, and began a brisk cannonade; upon which Captain Webber, of Captain Maxwell's brigade, brought two of his guns, and opened an admirable fire, which soon silenced them. The French behaved remarkably well, having stood to their guns until Webber completely dismounted them.

We were now most anxious to know how the battle was going on on the other side of the town. We therefore mounted the tops of the highest houses, and about three o'clock in the afternoon, with our glasses we could perceive, to our great delight, the bonnets of the gallant Highlanders of the Sixth Division, crowning the heights of the French position, and their batteries silenced. Soon after (an Easter Sunday that its inhabitants will long remember) closed the battle of Toulouse, and with it the Peninsular war, so long and so gloriously conducted by our illustrious leader. In this last exploit, we lost only three rank and file killed; Lieutenant Green severely, Lieutenants Clark and Deans slightly wounded, and twenty-four rank and file wounded. Poor Sergeant Munday, the orderly-room clerk, was sitting on a bank, a long way out of action, in the act of making out the return for the casualties, when a cannon-shot carried off one of his legs.

During the campaign, we had often experienced the most gentleman-like conduct from the French officers. A day or two before the battle, when we were upon our alarm post, at break of day, a fine hare was seen playing in a corn-field between the out-posts; a brace of greyhounds were very soon unslipped, when after an excellent course, poor puss was killed within the French lines. The officer to whom the dogs belonged, bowing to the French officer, called off the dogs; but the Frenchman politely sent the hare with a message, and his compliments, saying, that we required it more than they did.

On the 12th the French retired from Toulouse, and on the morning of the 13th, Sir Rowland's corps passed through and followed the enemy. The civility shown to us by the inhabitants of the city was surprising. Many of the officers were forced into the houses to partake of chocolate and fruit, while the ladies were pinning white cockades in our caps,—their joy was universal. We then advanced and were quartered in the village of Mongiscard. On the 14th, at an early hour, the British division of Sir Rowland's corps was congratulated by Sir Wm. Stewart, on dispatches having been received announcing Napoleon's abdication, thus putting an end to all further hostilities. Great was the joy expressed by all at this termination of our fatigues and dangers, and we reflected with thankfulness on our preservation through so many bloody actions, to return to our anxious friends, and native land. We moved forward, and on the 17th arrived at Ville Franche. Hostilities on the part of the French not having appeared to subside, in consequence of Marshal Soult not believing what had occurred, the troops therefore continued to stand to their arms an hour before daylight as usual. However, in the course of two or three days, we were glad to see Marshal Suchet, who had joined from Catalonia (a fine looking fellow), with General Gazan, the chief of Soult's staff, pass through our lines to visit Lord Wellington; but we were all much disappointed at not seeing Soult, particularly the men, as they wished very much to have a sight of "fighting Jack," or "the Duke of Damnation," as they called him. Every thing being settled, on the 22nd we retired to Villeneuve.

During the last ten months' fighting, from the 21st June, 1813, to the 10th April, 1814, we had, in killed and wounded, forty-three officers, twenty-seven sergeants, three drummers, and 731 rank and file.

On the 24th, we moved to Mongiscard, where we remained until the 4th of May, when we commenced a most delightful march to Bordeaux, through that beautiful country on the left bank of the Garonne. We arrived there on the 26th, and next day we encamped on the magnificent plain of Blanquefort, about five miles off, where we received orders to prepare to embark for America. Fortunately for us, our clothing had been lost in the Bay of Biscay, on its way out, and being in rags, we were ordered home, destined to reap more honourable laurels. On the 11th of June, we marched to Paulliac, and next day embarked on board the *Alfred* transport, when we dropped down the Garonne, and were transshipped to the *Ripon*, 74, Sir Christopher Cole, and sailed for Cork. In that magnificent harbour, after a delightful voyage, we arrived in the beginning of July, and on the 3rd, landed at East Ferry, highly gratified and delighted with the kind attention paid to us by Sir Christopher and his officers. As we immediately moved to Middleton, we all regretted we had not an opportunity of showing them any civility on shore; however, as a trifling acknowledgement, we had ordered in Cork, a handsome silver tureen, to be presented to the officers of the ward-room in our names; but unfortunately the *Ripon* was paid off, before it was completed.

On the 9th of July, we left Middleton for Birr, where we arrived on the 20th. We were now under the command of Major-General Beckwith, who had formerly been the adjutant of the regiment for many years, and had shared in many of their former achievements: he came to congratulate us on our return. We were now very busy in getting the regiment into order, which was soon done, and on the 4th of August we received orders to march to Fermoy, and to prepare for re-embarkation. We arrived there on the tenth of August, on the fifth of October we marched to Cork, and on the eighth we embarked at Monkstown, it was supposed, for America. An unfortunate accident occurred in getting on board one of the transports: an old soldier, Fox, of No. 6, fell overboard; and having his pack on, and his right arm through the sling of his firelock, he was carried down, and never seen afterwards. After laying in a sea stock to cross the Atlantic, we were disembarked on the 10th, and ordered to return to Cork barracks. On the 24th, the second battalion, stationed at Plymouth, was disbanded; the men and non-commissioned officers joined the 1st at Cork, on the 15th of November. The regiment again embarked in December, and after being a short time on board, returned a second time to Cork barracks.

## Chapter 10
# Waterloo

On the 26th of January we embarked a third time at Monkstown, being under orders to form part of that select little force under General Johnston, consisting of the 28th, 71st, 79th, 91st, and 92nd regiments, destined for Bermuda. We were detained in Cove, by contrary winds, until the 17th of March, when we sailed under convoy of the *Albion*; but in the afternoon, just as we were rounding Cape Clear, a frigate hove in sight, ordering us back, and telegraphing that Napoleon had escaped from Elba. We were quite delighted that our good fortune had not left us, and that we were thus saved a trip across the Atlantic. The regiments were ordered to different stations, the 28th to Warrenpoint, in the North of Ireland, where we landed, and marched through Newry, to Dundalk, where we arrived on the 23rd.

In the beginning of 1815, the Order of the Bath was enlarged. Our excellent commanding officer, Colonel Belson, was created a K.C.B. and likewise Brevet Lieutenant-Colonel Stovin, who was Sir Thomas Picton's adjutant-general, during the greater part of the Peninsular war, and had on many gallant occasions, proved an honour to "the Slashers."

We received orders, on the 24th of April, to march to Dublin, and embarked for Deal on the 27th, where we arrived on the 16th of May, after a tedious voyage up the channel. At Dublin, we went on board the transports from the quay, by planks. By some accident, as one of the old soldiers was going on board, the plank slipped, when he fell into the river, and was unfortunately drowned.

Our heavy baggage being landed, we proceeded next day to Ostend, where we arrived on the 18th, and on the 20th reached Ghent, by canal boats. Here we found Louis XVIII. in the old palace of Charles V.

On the 26th we moved on to Brussels. We were now in the finest order, fit for any service; but as poor as rats, having laid in stores three different times to cross the Atlantic, which were all thrown upon our hands.

On the 5th of June, the regiment was reviewed by the Duke of Wellington, on the Allée-Verte. When he came to the ground he warmly congratulated his old friends of the 28th, and expressed himself much pleased with their appearance. We now formed, with the 32nd, 79th, and part of the rifles, Sir James Kempt's brigade of the 5th division, under the gallant Picton.

On the afternoon of the 15th of June, several of the officers were walking in the park, when Sir Thomas Picton arrived. He came up to Sir Philip Belson, and desired to be introduced to the officers, saying he was. happy to have the 28th in his division: on the third day after this meeting, he died on the field of honour! Between nine and ten on that evening, the alarm was given, and the assembly sounded. The 5th division was soon formed round the park, where we remained upon our arms all night.

In the morning of the 16th, at four o'clock, the division left Brussels by the Porte de Namur; and marched in the direction of Genappe. We halted and breakfasted in the forest of Soigny, which was hardly finished, when a distant cannonade was heard. The division instantly fell in, and moved on in high spirits, to take its share in the battles of

Quatre Bras and Waterloo. The conduct of the 28th on the ever memorable Battle of Waterloo, and of the other regiments composing the 5th division, headed by the gallant and lamented Picton, cannot be better described than by extracting the paragraph from the admirable despatch of the conqueror of Napoleon:

> I must particularly mention the 28th, 42nd, 79th, and 92nd regiments, and the battalion of Hanoverians.[1]

As I have before said, mine is not a general history, but a record of the services of the regiment. I therefore know nothing more than others of the details of the action: I can only speak of our share in it, which was confined principally to repelling the furious charges of the enemy, and maintaining our position till the close of the day.

The coolness and intrepidity with which the regiment received and repulsed, in square, the several gallant charges of the enemy's cavalry, was the admiration of every one, and called forth the following short and soldier-like speech of the gallant Picton, who was in the centre:—

> Twenty-eighth, if I live to see the Prince Regent, I shall lay before him your bravery this day.

In one of the intervals between the attacks of the French cavalry on the 18th, that excellent officer, Lieutenant Irwin (now captain of grenadiers), went out with skirmishers, and was shot through the thigh. The cavalry again coming on, he with difficulty crawled in on his hands and knees, until he placed himself, as he considered, in perfect safety, under the bayonets of the kneeling ranks of those fine fellows.

In the actions the regiment suffered much:—on the 16th, we had eleven rank and file killed; four officers, Major Irving, Captain Bowles, Lieutenants Irwin and Coen, severely wounded, and four sergeants, and seventy-three rank and file. On the 18th, we had Major Mitcham killed upon the spot, and one sergeant, and twenty-four rank and file. Lieutenants Ingram and Clark, were mortally wounded; Lieutenant-colonel Nixon, Major Llewllyn, Captain English, Lieutenants Wilkinson, Gilbert, Eason, Skelton, Bridgeland, and Ensign Mount-Steven severely, Captain Kelly, Lieutenants Hilliard, Carrothers, and Deans, slightly. In Mitcham we suffered a great loss, he was a most gallant fellow; he was shot through the heart, and fell dead. Mitcham had fought in the ranks of the regiment as an officer from his youth; he had been born in it; and had distinguished himself in Egypt, and on many other occasions. His father had been formerly paymaster. Poor Ingram had distinguished himself at Albuera, with the 2nd battalion; one of his legs was shattered by a cannon shot. He suffered amputation on the field, and a second time at Brussels; and but for an unfortunate accident, he might probably have been saved; the tourniquet shifted during the night, and he bled to death,—his room next morning was found deluged with blood.

The case of that excellent officer, Lieutenant Clarke, was truly distressing. The splinter of a shell had uncovered his bowels. He was carried to Brussels, where he survived for two or three days, perfectly conscious of his dreadful situation; but with manliness and resignation submitted to his fate, in the same serenity of temper which had always endeared him to his brother officers, until mortification coming on, put an end to his sufferings. He died in the arms of his messmates, Lieutenants Gilbert and Shelton[2].

In the action of the 18th, a division of the French having been repulsed with the loss of eagles, Lieutenant Deans, of the regiment, hurried away by his enthusiasm, accompanied the cavalry in the pursuit on foot; he attacked sword in hand every Frenchman that came in his way, and had cut

2. They were all three much regretted. A plain marble slab in the church of Waterloo, erected by their brother officers, records their glorious death.

down two, and wounded several, when being overpowered he was taken prisoner, and stripped of his entire clothing, except his shirt, in which state he joined the regiment next day, the 19th, severely wounded.

On the 19th we advanced, and followed the retreating enemy by Neville. On the afternoon of the 20th we bivouacked on the field of the battle of Malplaquet, where the 28th (then Viscount Mordaunt's regiment), under the great Marlborough, had shared in the glories of that day, on the 11th September, 1709. Sir Philip Belson having obtained the command of the brigade, I now succeeded to the command of the regiment. We then moved upon Paris.

On the 8th July we reached St. Denis,—some of the fugitive French were still there; but they retired next day. On the 10th we moved forward, and encamped near the village of Clichy, on the banks of the Seine, about two miles from Paris. We were so fortunate as to have again attached to our division (the fifth) our excellent chaplain, (of the Second Division, during the Peninsular campaign,) the Reverend Charles Frith, whose humane conduct on the heights of Maya has already been recorded. On the Sunday after our arrival at Clichy, the division paraded for divine service, the first time since the battle of the 18th, in the park of the château (Sir James Kempt's quarters), when Mr. Frith gave us an impressive discourse. The text, as well as I can recollect, was—"Go to your tents and rejoice, and return thanks to the Lord for the mercies he has granted you."

The beautiful manner in which he dwelt on the battle, and the sad and sudden loss of friends and comrades, drew tears from many; and when he wound up with the sad pangs it would cause at home, to the widows and orphans, the parents and friends of those that had fallen, concluding with the text, "Go to your tents and rejoice, and return thanks to the Lord for the mercies he has granted you," there was hardly a dry eye in the whole division, and it had an excellent effect on the men.

Sir John Kean getting the command of the brigade, Sir C. P. Belson was appointed to the third division. On the 20th July, Colonel Sir C. Belson took leave of the regiment[3], which he had so long commanded with honour to himself, and beloved by every body under him, in the following regimental order:

> Regimental Order
>
> Colonel Sir Philip Belson, being appointed to the staff of the army, and removed to the third division, cannot resign the command of the 28th Regiment, at the head of which corps he has had the honour of being placed above ten years, without experiencing the deepest regret; and he begs Captain Cadell, now in charge of it, the officers, and men, will accept his warmest thanks for the zeal and alacrity with which they have invariably seconded his efforts in the performance of his duty upon so many trying and distinguished occasions; and at the same time he assures them that it ever will be with feelings of the utmost pride and pleasure that he looks back to the period of his life when he had the happiness of having them under his command.
>
> *C. P. Belson*
>
> Colonel and Lieutenant-Colonel. 28th Regt.
>
> Paris
>
> 20th July, 1815

---

3. I received the following letter from Sir Charles Philip Belson on this occasion:

Paris

20th July, 1815

*My dear Cadell,*

I request you will do me the favour of putting the enclosed into your orderly book. It is the only feeble means I possess (continued on next page)

The allied armies having now joined, Paris was soon in our possession; and on the 24th July the whole of the British army was formed in contiguous close columns on the great road from Paris to Neuilly. At 12 o'clock the allied sovereigns arrived, and rode down the front; We then moved from the right, and in quarter-distance columns marched down the Champ Elysées, where we had the honour of marching past them, they having taken up their posts in the Place Louis Quinze. When the 28th passed, the Duke was seen to point them out. The men were still in their ragged clothes; the colour-staffs were shot to pieces; one of them was two yards long, the other only one. I had afterwards the satisfaction of marching the regiment through the capital of France, and returned to the camp. We could only then muster four companies.

By the beginning of August the quartermaster, who had been sent to Deal for the new clothing, returned, when the "Slashers" very soon resumed their usual appearance. About the middle of August the whole of the British army was collected on the plains of St Dennis, where the Duke exhibited to the allied sovereigns the evolutions of one of his most splendid achievements, the battle of Salamanca. The Emperor Alexander paid particular attention to the 28th, and admired much the grenadier company. He was

---

of expressing what I suffer on parting with my friends of every rank in the 28th Regiment, where I entered as commanding officer above ten years ago, and where I have experienced some of the happiest days of my life, which I can never hope to see renewed. I have not said much, for no words of mine—and I think you will believe me sincere—can convey my feelings upon the present occasion.

You will oblige me much by consulting with the mess what sort of article would be acceptable to them; for amongst them I aspire to be remembered, and place a token of my esteem and regard for my officers, whose society I am about to lose, but never, I hope, their friendship.

Believe me, always
Yours and theirs faithfully,
*C. P. Belson*
Captain Cadell
Commanding 28th Regt, Clichy

much pleased with our brown calf-skin packs, and after minutely examining one, asked their origin. He laughed much when I told him that they were found in a French store we took in Egypt.

We remained on the banks of the Seine until the 28th of October, when most of our officers had their tents pitched in the delightful gardens of Clichy. The gardener of that which our officers occupied, having been very civil, we made a collection of old clothes for him, amongst which Lieutenant Hilliard contributed a pair of old boots: what was the gardener's surprise on looking at them, to find that they had belonged to his own master ! and we were not a little astonished, when we found that we had encamped in the garden of General Brune, who was taken prisoner at the surprise of Arroyo del Molinos in October 1811.

On the 29th of October, the camp on the banks of the Seine was broken up, when we marched to St. Germaine, and on the 31st reached Vigny, where we were cantoned in the neighbouring villages. The grenadier company occupied the château of Marshal Grouchy. About the end of November, the 28th, with the Highland regiments, which had suffered so much at Waterloo, were ordered to return to England; we commenced our march on the 1st of November, and arrived at Calais on the 16th. On our way down the country, the men suffered much from the excessive cold, particularly some of the Highlanders, their kilts, having frozen, cut them severely. We embarked, and sailed the following day: the transports were dispersed in a storm, but were all fortunate enough to make Dover or Margate in safety. We proceeded to Hilsea, where we re-united on the 27th. About this time, we lost our excellent colonel, the veteran General Robert Prescott, so distinguished for his services in the West Indies. He was succeeded by Sir Edward Paget, who had led the 28th as lieutenant-colonel, on many a gallant occasion.

## Chapter 11
# Islands in the Mediterranean

1816. On the 13th of January, 1816, we moved to Haslar; and on the 11th of April received that enviable distinction, the Waterloo medal, which was distributed to officers, non-commissioned officers, and men, for their services on that memorable day.

About this time, that gallant officer, Colonel Browne, whose name is so often honourably mentioned in this narrative, assumed the command of the regiment, having exchanged from the 56th, Sir Philip Belson being on the eve of promotion to the rank of major-general, Brevet Lieutenant-Colonel Sir Frederick Stovin succeeded Brevet Lieutenant-Colonel Nixon in the majority. About the end of May, we removed to the new barracks at Forton.

The first anniversary of the battle of Waterloo, was commemorated by the presentation of a splendid stand of colours, sent to the regiment by Sir Edward Paget, for whom Colonel Browne officiated in the following manner.

At noon, the regiment was paraded as strong as possible, and formed into a hollow square, rank entire, with "ordered arms," and unfixed bayonets. The colours were brought out, and after an excellent speech from the colonel, at his word of command, the men drew and kissed their bayonets, and then swearing to stand to their colours, saluted them. The officers did the same with their swords, and the band played "God save the king." At Colonel Browne's command, bayonets were fixed, and shouldered, the men presented arms, the band again playing the national anthem, when three cheers closed this interesting ceremony. To celebrate this glorious day still further, the officers entertained at dinner Lord Howard of Effingham, and the staff of the district: his lordship, as Major-general Howard, had commanded a brigade of the Second Division, on many distinguished occasions.

We remained at Forton until the beginning of December, 1817, when we embarked for Malta, at which island, after a delightful voyage, we arrived on the 15th; and in the spring of 1818, the regiment went up to Corfu.

1819. Early in 1819, the regiment was detached to Zante, Cephalonia, and Santa Maura, and returned to Corfu the August following, leaving Sir Frederick Stovin at Santa Maura, with 200 men, and fifteen artillerymen. About the end of September, a spirit of insurrection commenced among the natives of Santa Maura: headed by their priests, they assembled 1,500 well-armed peasantry, and threatened to burn the houses of the inhabitants of the town, who were obnoxious to them. Sir Frederick Stovin kept them at bay with his small force, held the fort, and protected the town, until he reported to Corfu, when the light companies of the 28th and 32nd were sent down.

On the afternoon of the 3rd of October, the Greeks seeing the transports with the reinforcements coming, made a rush with their whole force into the town, drove in a small picquet of the 28th, wounded several, and killed an artilleryman. On the light companies landing, the natives were driven back, when they took up a strong position at the village of Spachiotes, about three miles distant.

On the 4th, Sir Frederick Stovin advanced with the

light infantry, drove them from their strong hold, and took possession of the village. The 28th and 32nd were led in the most gallant manner by Captain Kelly and Major Crowe:—several of their priests were taken, tried, and executed, which completely suppressed the rebellion. The 28th had several men wounded, and one missing, who was never afterwards heard of. Sir Frederick, for his judicious conduct, was created a knight of St. Michael and St. George. Lieutenant Monroe, of the 32nd, had a narrow escape: on advancing to the village, a Greek snapped a pistol close at him, and was about to repeat the act, when Sergeant Taylor, of the 28th, rushed forward, and drove his bayonet and half his fusee through his body. The grenadiers of the 8th and 28th arrived on the morning of the 5th, but the business was all over, although no time had been lost by them; for it was not until seven p. m., on the 4th, that the order was sent by Sir Frederick Adam, from the old palace of Corfu, to Fort Neuf, where they were quartered, and in the short space of twenty-five minutes they were afloat in gunboats, in heavy marching order. Sir F. Adams was highly pleased with their alertness.

Some time after the execution of the priests, there was much drunkenness prevailing among the troops, and as they had very little money, it could not be accounted for, until a grenadier of the 8th was brought to a court martial. On his sentence being read, Sir F. Stovin said he would forgive him if he told the cause of the drunkenness, when the following laughable story came out:—He had purchased a quantity of rope, of the size used at the executions, and sold it for a quarter-dollar an inch to the deluded natives, as relics of the ropes which had hung their priests!

1828. The regiment remained in the Ionian Islands until the end of 1828, when they embarked, and arrived at Cork in March, 1829, whence they joined the depôt at

Buttevant. During the summer, the regiment was reviewed by Sir John Byng, the Commander of the Forces, and Sir George Bingham: they both expressed themselves highly pleased. In October the regiment received a route for Newry; but it was afterwards changed for Galway. About the end of 1829, and the beginning of 1830, the west of Ireland was becoming very much disturbed. In the middle of February, therefore, a moveable column of two companies of the 28th, accompanied by Lieutenant McNamara, and a party of the 8th Hussars, under my command, left Galway for the county of Mayo, whence they returned after tranquillity had been restored.

In the beginning of March, the "Terry Alt" war broke out in the counties of Galway and Clare; on the 16th of March, I was dispatched with two companies of my regiment, and a squadron of the 8th Hussars and the 6th Inniskillen Dragoons, to Gort, and took the command of the garrison. During four months, we experienced some of the most unpleasant and harassing duty in which troops can be engaged, having had to perform continued day and night marches of sixteen and eighteen hours, after the unfortunate and deluded peasantry. The troops employed on this arduous service, performed their duty with so much steadiness and good temper, that they received the thanks of the Marquis of Anglesea on the occasion, handsomely conveyed to them through the commander of the district:

> Ennis
> 31st May, 1831
> *Sir*,—In transmitting the accompanying district order, Major-General Sir Thomas Arbuthnot desires me to assure you, that he fully appreciates the zeal and activity you have evinced in the execution of the various duties you have been called upon to perform, and the support he has at all times received from you.

I have the honour to be, Sir,
Your obedient, humble servant,
Charles Corkran
Major Cadell
A. D. C.
Commanding at Gort

District Order
Ennis
30th May, 1831
No. 1.—Major-General Sir Thomas Arbuthnot, has the utmost satisfaction in informing the troops stationed in Clare and the disturbed parts of Galway, that in consequence of the very favourable reports made by the Lieutenant-general commanding, to the Irish government, the Lord Lieutenant has been pleased to command, that his Excellency's sentiments on the subject should be made known to the troops alluded to in the strongest terms; and the Major-General feels, that he cannot do so more forcibly, than by promulgating the following extract from the Lord Lieutenant's letter to him on the subject, *viz.*—

> And you cannot express in too strong terms to the officers and troops acting under your orders, my high estimation of their zeal, energy, patience, and forbearance.

No. 2.—With reference to reports made by Majors Cadell and Waring, of the 28th and 59th regiments, relative to the assemblage of troops in the vicinity of Derrybrien, and the Major-General's own report respecting the admirable good conduct of the troops lately assembled on various occasions near Ballinacally, &c, for the execution of extensive arrests, the lieutenant-general commanding has directed, that a communication shall be made to the officers, non-commissioned officers, and privates, employed on those occasions, of his admiration of the accuracy and discipline with which the service was conducted.

No. 3.—It now remains for the major-general to return to the officers in charge of regimental detachments, and all those under their immediate command, his most sincere thanks for the manner in which they have on all occasions supported him; and in expressing a hope, that the discipline and good conduct of the troops, which has been hitherto so conspicuous, may be strictly kept up in future, he is anxious to avail himself of this opportunity to entreat, that in their endeavours to arrest those concerned in the atrocious outrages daily committed in this country, and who should be followed unremittingly, the officers and non-commissioned officers will not fail constantly to point out to the small sinners and peasantry in general, that the military force has been sent to this country for their protection, as well as to render assistance to the civil power.

By order
Charles Corkran
A. D. C.

To be communicated to the detachments under your command.

Major Cadell, C. C.
Commanding at Gort

Early in October, the regiment was ordered to Dublin[1], and in the beginning of March, 1832, our excellent colo-

1. On tranquillity being restored, the principal inhabitants of Gort and the neighbourhood, presented me with a handsome hand-salver, to testify their opinion of my services as a magistrate and commander of the garrison of Gort.

nel, Sir Edward Paget, gave the regiment a handsome stand of colours, which were consecrated on the 19th of March, and presented by his brother, His Excellency the Marquis of Anglesea, at Dublin Castle, of which the best account that can be given is an extract from the *Dublin Times.*

**The Marquis of Anglesea—the 28th Regiment**

We give in another column the particulars of the consecration and presentation of a new stand of colours to the 28th Regiment. The speech delivered by his Excellency the Marquis of Anglesea on the occasion, presents a highly animated though brief description of the various scenes in which this gallant regiment distinguished itself. It affords in fact an epitome of the modern military history of the empire, which will be read with intense interest by every soldier, and with feelings of pride and gratification by every lover of his country.

The new colours, inclosed in their cases, were escorted by a guard of honour, composed of the grenadier company of the regiment, from the barracks to the chapel of the castle, at the entrance of which they were uncased, and then placed one on each side of the altar. The sergeant-major and colour-sergeants mounted sentry over them at the chapel door; and as soon as his Excellency the Lord Lieutenant, accompanied by his family and household, had entered and taken their places (the grenadiers and light company of the 28th Regiment being also present), the Reverend C. Vignobles read the morning service, at the conclusion of which he performed the ceremony of the consecration in the usual form.

The colours were then recased, and delivered to Majors Cadell and Crole—the senior major, with the king's colour, to the right—the junior, with the regimental colour, being on the left; and in this order, escorted by the guard of honour, proceeded to the upper castle-yard, when the battalion was drawn up, forming three sides of a square facing inwards, and the centre fronting the portico.

His Excellency, dressed in the splendid uniform of the 7th Hussars (his own regiment), and mounted on his favourite charger, then appeared, and was received with the usual salute of arms and colours, after which he addressed the regiment in the following words:

> Twenty-eighth!
>
> A more pleasing task could not have been imposed upon me than that of presenting colours to this distinguished regiment.
>
> Such a ceremony is always interesting; but this is peculiarly so to me from the following circumstances:
>
> First. It is the first battalion with which I ever brigaded, having been placed, with the regiment I had raised in 1793, under the command of General Lord Cathcart, whose brigade then consisted of the 27th, 28th, 80th, and 84th Regiments.
>
> Secondly. This celebrated regiment was commanded by my excellent brother, your present colonel, but then its lieutenant-colonel.
>
> Were I to dwell upon all the exploits of this gallant corps, the recital would be tedious; nor is it necessary that I should do so, for the old soldiers, no doubt, keep up the good old custom of relating the achievements of themselves, and of those who preceded them, and thus the young men of the regiment are always pretty well acquainted with its history.

However, I cannot refrain from touching lightly upon some of the most remarkable incidents of your career of glory.

I cannot fix the exact period at which the 28th Regiment was raised; however, I find it engaged in the wars of Marlborough, and it served with that great captain from 1704 to 1709. That it was much distinguished, and frequently noticed in dispatches, and thanked in orders.

In 1759 I find it engaged with the immortal Wolfe. That excellent general—that model of an officer—was killed at the storming of the lines of Quebec, whilst leading on the 28th Regiment.

I need not relate the result of that day. The 28th were advancing—the victory was certain.

The 28th were employed during the greater part of the subsequent American war upon that continent, and maintained their high name.

In the French revolutionary war the 28th were also much employed. In 1794 they formed part of a corps, under the command of the Earl of Moira, which was encamped near Southampton. It became of great importance to reinforce his Royal Highness the Duke of York, then commanding the British and Hanoverian troops in Flanders. Earl Moira, since Marquis of Hastings, landed with his little army at Ostend, and by a skilful and rapid movement eluded the vigilance of the French army, purposely placed to intercept them, and successfully joined his Royal Highness. It was then I first became acquainted with the 28th, and I soon began to admire them. I will not dwell upon all the details of the severe winter campaign which ensued. I will merely relate a few facts which came under my own observation.

The 28th was severely engaged in the sortie at Nimeguen. The French works were stormed, and their batteries destroyed. The position, however, of the armies made it necessary to retreat, and in this long retreat the 28th had various opportunities of distinguishing itself, although no great battle was fought.

I well remember one handsome exploit. Lord Cathcart's corps was in position at Buesin. The 27th had an advanced post at the village Guildermansel, where there was a small river and bridge.

This brave battalion had been seriously attacked all day—it became necessary to reinforce it—the 28th was ordered to advance—they formed in front of the 27th, taking up the line of the border of the river, and immediately opened a well-directed, uninterrupted, rolling fire for twenty-five minutes. They totally dislodged the corps opposed to them, and remained the unmolested masters of the post.

The retreat, however, continued; but I can make this assertion, that although from the defection of our allies, and from overwhelming numbers, it was impossible to make a permanent stand, yet throughout the whole campaign there did not occur a single instance in which the British did not beat the enemy on the field of battle.

I also well remember an order of General Lord Cathcart's, upon the occasion of his detaching, for a particular service, the 27th and 28th Regiments. It ran thus—"Whenever danger is to be apprehended, and difficulties are to be encountered, the 27th and 28th Regiments are sure to be called upon," &c.; and true it is they were never called for in vain.

There is one characteristic of the regiment I am now addressing, which I advert to with the greatest pleasure.

Whatever were its difficulties, however it was harassed or distressed, it always turned out stronger than any other corps. I appeal to the gallant general before me, if this is not one of the most valuable qualities of a regiment.

Hospitals were their aversion. Their home was their battalion, and they were never happy away from it. In those days the commissariat and the hospital establishments had not arrived at that perfection they have since attained.

It was commonly said by commanding officers, that you might as well kill a man in the field as send him to a general hospital: he was at least lost to the battalion for the campaign.

Not so the 28th. These poor ragged fellows (for they had lost their new clothing), whatever had been their casualties, they were always crawling back to their home—their battalion.

You saw them in small groups, deserting, as it were, from the hospital, helping each other along—half naked indeed, but always bringing with them their arms, and in high order. The locks were clean—the bayonets were sharp. Finally, this regiment embarked for England.

Their next exploit was the reduction of Minorca, under General Sir Charles Stewart—Lieutenant-Colonel Paget always at their head.

They then went to Egypt

The landing of the army on the 8th March, under General Sir Ralph Abercrombie, was the most brilliant and imposing sight that ever was beheld. It was gallantly opposed. The 28th was one of the first regiments that formed on the beach. They drove all before them—cavalry, infantry, and guns. A position was taken up in advance; in it the army was furiously assailed at the dawn of the day, on the 21st of March. The 28th occupied an ancient ruin, with scarcely any cover in front, and entirely open on the flanks and rear. Having repulsed the first front attack of cavalry, they were again assailed in front, flanks, and rear.

The simple order given was—"Rear-ranks, about—fire!" Not a man gave way, and the enemy was totally repulsed.

On this day the good, the gallant, the amiable Abercrombie fell—regretted, deeply regretted by all.

Subsequently the army advanced upon Cairo, which they reduced, making 10,000 prisoners.

Finally, the British army having expelled the French from Egypt, was withdrawn from it. The 28th was next employed at the reduction of Copenhagen, and after that formed part of an expedition to Sweden under Sir John Moore. It returned to Portsmouth, and without disembarking was pushed on to Portugal, to reinforce the Duke of Wellington, then Sir A. Wellesley. It was not, however, in time to partake of the brilliant affair of Vimiera and Roleia, which he achieved.

The army then advanced, and took possession of Lisbon, and by a convention the French troops evacuated Portugal. General Sir John Moore was now sent to command in that country. The 28th formed part of his army.

It having been determined that an attempt should be made to relieve Spain, a corps under Sir David Baird was sent to Corunna, to advance through the Gallicias, whilst Sir John Moore should move forward from Portugal.

A junction was formed at Toro. I well remember it; it was an interesting moment to me. I had the advanced guard of the former column; my brother that of Sir John Moore. Our patrols fell in with each other, and I soon found myself in the presence of General Paget and his faithful 28th, which formed part of the reserve which he commanded. The whole, with the cavalry, were then placed at my disposal.

The army advanced before Sahagun. A battle was to be fought; but general the Marquis de la Romana having announced the total inefficiency of his Spanish army, and his inability to second the efforts of Sir John Moore, it became necessary to fall back upon Corunna.

Whilst in the plains, the cavalry covered the movements of the army; when within the mountains, the infantry took the rear guard.

Battle was offered at Lugo, but the enemy did not attack. The retreat was continued. In front of Corunna a position was taken up, in which we were attacked. The enemy was beaten.

A masterly movement of General Paget with the reserve (the 28th of course belonged to it) mainly contributed to this result He turned the left flank of the enemy, and they retreated. Here, in the presence of the regiment, the brave, the favourite Moore fell;—here he was consigned to the grave! The army embarked. In 1809 the 28th was of the expedition to Walcheren. Flushing was reduced. The same year it was sent again to Portugal, and a part of it was at the celebrated passage of the Douro (where General Paget lost his arm), and at the taking of Oporto.

Time will not admit of my entering into a detail of all the glorious exploits of the regiment in the Peninsula; suffice it to say, that it bore a very conspicuous part in most of the great battles won there by the Duke of Wellington.

It was at Talavera, at Busaco, Torres Vedras, Albuera, Barossa (the gallant achievement of General Lord Lynedoch), Arroyo del Molino, Almaraz, Vittoria, the several battles of the Pyrenees, the passage of the Nivelle, of the Nive, at Orthes, at Toulouse. It closed the war at Waterloo. It had been closely engaged on the sixteenth of June at Quatre Bras, where it repulsed a furious attack of the French cuirassiers. Throughout the whole of the eighteenth, it was incessantly engaged at Waterloo; again, in its presence the gallant Picton fell! One trait I cannot resist adverting to. There were periods in that great day at which the army was much pressed and overwhelmed by numbers. I saw a battalion in square falling back, but in the most perfect order. I rode up and asked what battalion it was? "The 28th, my Lord," said the gallant Belson, who had long served with distinction in it, and who had belonged to my regiment.

I instantly said "You are the very fellows I want: go, form in that position, and you shall be immediately supported." They cheerfully obeyed the call: they deployed, stopped the enemy, and held their station. The result of the day is universally known : I need not dwell upon it

Twenty-eighth! I have now brought you to the close of your glorious war. Glorious, indeed, and truly fortunate it has been. It would seem as if you had been predestined to form a guard of honour to our illustrious slain. Wolfe was killed at your head — Abercrombie died in your presence—Moore fell by your side—you witnessed the death of the gallant Picton, who had so often led you to victory!

Twenty-eighth! You began your career under the incomparable Marlborough! You have finished the war under the immortal Wellington. I consign your colours to your charge. I do it in the most perfect confidence. Whatever may be your destination, in whatever clime or country you may serve, I know you will bear them to honour and to glory. Twenty-eighth ! May success ever attend you!'

A general and enthusiastic burst of applause, from the crowd assembled in the castle-yard, testified their admiration of this animated and truly soldier-like address, whilst every officer and private of this gallant regiment, although restrained by the rules of military discipline from giving utterance to their feelings, shewed by their proud and martial bearing, (and a finer body of men never bore arms in the service of their country) how highly they prized the well-earned fame of their brave corps.

His Excellency having delivered the new colours to Ensigns Wodehouse and Hailes, received the old standards from them, which he handed to the majors, who stood in attendance to receive them. Lieutenant-Colonel Hailes then addressed his Excellency, as follows:

> My Lord,
>
> The honour you have this day conferred on the 28th Regiment, is deeply felt by every individual composing the corps; and for them and in their behalf and my own, I beg to tender you our best acknowledgements.
>
> The gallant and noble name of Paget has long been associated with this regiment, as well as with the brightest page of the military history of the country. The recollection of this day will not the less cherish the feelings borne by us all towards your house; and I will add, that the colours which your Excellency has now entrusted to our keeping, shall be defended as honourably, and with the same courage and constancy, as those hitherto borne by the 28th.

Early in the summer of 1832, the regiment left Dublin, and was detached in the Queen's County, Kildare, and Wicklow. About the end of July the regiment again moved to Fermoy, and in the end of November to Cork.

1833. During the spring of 1833, the 28th was several times employed on that most disagreeable of duties,—the protection of tithe proctors: on these occasions their soldier-like conduct procured them the thanks of Major-general Sir Thomas Arbuthnot. In July the regiment moved to Limerick, and at the end of 1833 crossed over to England.

## Chapter 12

# The Services of the Second Battalion

1809. The second battalion of the 28th Regiment remained in Ireland until June 1809, when it embarked at Cork for Lisbon, under the command of Lieutenant-colonel the Hon. Alexander Abercrombie, forming part of a reinforcement of 3000 for Lord Wellington's army, under General Lighthume. The fleet, convoyed by the *Virginia* frigate, arrived at Lisbon, after a fine passage of six days, on the 30th of June. The troops disembarked the following day at Belem, and were encamped near Lisbon, with the 5th Regiment, which had arrived from England. The light brigade, consisting of the 43rd, 52nd, and 95th, marched on the 4th of July to join the army, then understood to be moving upon Talavera de la Reyna, where they arrived the morning after the action. But the troops recently arrived, consisting of the 2nd battalion of the 28th, 34th, 39th, 42nd, and 92nd Regiments, not being able to complete their equipments, did not leave Lisbon until the 22nd or 23rd of July, when they embarked in boats, and ascended the Tagus as far as Santarem. Thence they moved by Abrantes and Castello Branco, towards the Spanish frontier,—the 2nd battalions of the 28th, 42nd, and 92nd, being brigaded together under that excellent officer Brigadier-General Catlin Crawford.[1]

On reaching Zarza Mayor, intelligence reached them of the battle of Talavera, and of the movement of the army under Lord Wellington, upon the Guadiana. General Crawford's brigade was therefore ordered to move in the direction of Elvas, but on their arrival at Niza, was halted there, and encamped for three weeks. Having no tents, the young officers and soldiers, unaccustomed to bivouack in the open air, here suffered severely from fever and ague. In the beginning of September, the brigade marched through Elvas, and joined the main body of the army in cantonments on the Guadiana, at Montigo de la Calzada, and the neighbouring villages on both sides of the river. Here a new arrangement was made, the second battalions of the 28th, 34th, and 39th, being sent as a brigade to join Lieutenant-General Hill's division, and the second battalions of the 42nd and 92nd, being ordered to join their first battalion. The division under General Hill, after breaking up from cantonments in Estremadura, passed by Badajos and Niza, to the neighbourhood of Abrantes, the 2d battalion 28th being quartered for some time in the village of Sardial. In the beginning of 1810, the division moved towards Castello Branco, where they remained some time watching the *corps d'armée* under the Count D'Erlon.

In September 1810, the 2nd, 28th, formed part of General Hill's division, when he executed that rapid and able march to the support of Lord Wellington at Busaco, where they joined the right of the line and partook of the glory of that action. The army afterwards retiring to the lines of

---

1. ( See previous page) The gallant Highlanders and the 28th were often destined to serve together during the war, and these three fine corps of young soldiers were each commanded by Scottish officers of distinguished families. The brave but unfortunate Lord Blantyre led the 42nd, Abercrombie the 28th, and Lamont the 92nd. Upon their separation, the young Highlanders gained their first laurels in the field of Fuentes d' Honor, and the 28th in that of Albuera.

Torres Vedras, the 2nd battalion 28th were posted in the village of Bucellas, celebrated for its wine[2].

The 2nd battalion 28th crossed the Tagus with General Hill, and were cantoned at Almeyrim, opposite to the enemy's head-quarters. On the retreat of Marshal Massena, they formed part of the 2nd division in its movements on the frontiers, and assisted in the expulsion of the French from Campo Major; whence they crossed the Guadiana, and after several affairs of smaller importance, formed part of the army that invested Badajos on the second of May, 1811. In consequence of the advance of Marshal Soult the siege was raised on the 14th of May, when they marched to Albuera, and shared in that memorable but dearly bought victory, in which these young soldiers well maintained, by their gallantry, the character of the corps to which they belonged, under the command of Major (afterwards Lieutenant-Colonel) Paterson, the Hon. Colonel Abercrombie having succeeded to the command of the brigade. In this action the 2nd battalion 28th suffered very severely; and their conduct procured them on this, as well as on other occasions, the thanks of that excellent officer, Major-General the Honourable William Stewart.

---

2. Almost every other house in the town was a wine-store, and immense vats and tuns, containing many hogsheads each, were to be found even in the rooms occupied by officers and men; far too great a temptation to put in the way of soldiers, as the following anecdote will prove. The officers of our light company, having given a wine party, to which some brother officers were invited, had found, when rather too late in the evening, the stock of wine which they had laid in for the occasion to be exhausted; upon which the junior subaltern was requested to proceed with a camp kettle to the vat for a fresh supply, as it was so excellent. On turning the cock, and finding no wine to run, the vat was pronounced dry. However, it was determined to make another attempt by letting down the camp kettle by a rope through a trap door in the top of the vat. Still finding it not return replenished, but rather that some obstacle interposed, the officer procured a lamp to examine the interior, when to his horror, the first object that presented itself was a British drummer, in full regimentals, pack, haversack and all, floating in the wine, who had been missing for some days, and was supposed to have deserted! "Drummer wine" was long a bye-word with us.

At the battle of Albuera we had Captains Gale and Carroll, Lieutenants Crummer, Cottingham, and Shelton, and Ensign Ingram, wounded.—After going into cantonments for some time on the frontiers, they joined our first battalion at Villa Viciosa, in August, 1811, and on the 24th of that month the men were incorporated with the first battalion, whilst the officers and non-commissioned officers were sent home as a skeleton battalion, after receiving the thanks of both General Hill and the commander-in-chief, for their gallantry and good conduct, as already related in the narrative of the first battalion. During the remainder of the war they were stationed principally at Berryhead, in Devonshire, whence they furnished excellent supplies of officers and men, to fill the gaps made afterwards in our first battalion in many a hard-fought field; and in 1814, at the close of the war, were reduced, with the other 2nd battalions of the army.

About the middle of 1826 we lost our much-respected and gallant brother officer, Lieutenant-Colonel Irving. From the severity of his wounds, both arms had been nearly disabled, and this, together with the impaired state of his health, obliged him finally to retire from the service.

In September, 1827, the 28th suffered a severe loss in the retirement of their gallant commanding officer, Colonel John Frederick Browne, C.B. He had served in the regiment since 1784 or 85, with the exception of between three and four years, after his promotion to the 56th.

It would be endless to mention the many places at which he distinguished himself. His career as a soldier was marked by gallantry on every occasion—Holland, in 1794—the West Indies—the capture of Minorca—Egypt—Tariffa—Barossa—Flanders! He was succeeded by Lieutenant-Colonel Hailes.

1828. For several years, during our stay in the Ionian Islands, Captain Crummer had the important command of the Island of Calamos. That island was appointed for the reception of the Greek women and children who fled thither to escape Turkish barbarity.

The captain's command was attended with no ordinary difficulty, as may be inferred, when we consider that he had not less than 9,000 women to keep in order.

This excellent officer performed a most important service just before the battle of Albuera. The fusilier brigade was detached. He was sent off, with the small escort of two Portuguese dragoons, to bring up the brigade. He succeeded in avoiding the enemy's outposts, and brought them up to perform their glorious part in that desperate action.

An excellent picture was presented to the regiment, in the spring of 1833, by Lieutenant-Colonel Charles Hamilton Smith (drawn by himself), representing the 28th in square, repelling the attack of the French cavalry on the 16th, which hangs in the mess-room.

The 28th are the only instance in the army of being allowed to bear a most honourable badge—the number on the back of their caps— in consequence of their coolness and intrepidity in Egypt on the memorable 21st. They were attacked in front by infantry, and in the rear by cavalry; the rear ranks went to the right about, when they defeated both columns.

Our late commanding officer, Sir Charles Philip Belson, during the Peninsular war, instituted two badges of merit amongst the non-commissioned officers of the regiment Whenever new clothing came out, there were always a number of embroidered crowns and stars. The crown he gave for gallantry in the field, and the star for steady good conduct in quarters. They were worn above the chevrons. The emulation it caused and the good it did were very great; it was considered a terrible disgrace if anything occurred to deprive any one of his badge of honour.

In 1824, Sir C. P. Belson presented the regiment with a superb snuff-box, composed of silver medals struck to commemorate their actions.

That promising young officer, Lieutenant Gordon, who was killed at Lembege, on the 18th of March, 1814, being adjutant to the light company, was mounted on a very fine French mare, which had been captured at the surprise of Arroyo Molinos; when he fell, she faced the heavy fire, and galloped in amongst her old masters.

In October, 1834, the 28th moved from Manchester to Chatham, where I now take leave of them, preparing to embark for New South Wales, and from thence to the East, where they will unfurl their banners, covered with their gallant actions, with the same credit to themselves and honour to their country, they have so nobly done in Europe for the last thirty years.

# ALSO FROM LEONAUR

**AVAILABLE IN SOFTCOVER OR HARDCOVER WITH DUST JACKET**

**CAPTAIN OF THE 95th (Rifles)** *by Jonathan Leach*—An officer of Wellington's Sharpshooters during the Peninsular, South of France and Waterloo Campaigns of the Napoleonic Wars.

**BUGLER AND OFFICER OF THE RIFLES** *by William Green & Harry Smith* With the 95th (Rifles) during the Peninsular & Waterloo Campaigns of the Napoleonic Wars

**BAYONETS, BUGLES AND BONNETS** by *James 'Thomas' Todd*—Experiences of hard soldiering with the 71st Foot - the Highland Light Infantry - through many battles of the Napoleonic wars including the Peninsular & Waterloo Campaigns

**THE ADVENTURES OF A LIGHT DRAGOON** *by George Farmer & G.R. Gleig*—A cavalryman during the Peninsular & Waterloo Campaigns, in captivity & at the siege of Bhurtpore, India

**THE COMPLEAT RIFLEMAN HARRIS** *by Benjamin Harris as told to & transcribed by Captain Henry Curling*—The adventures of a soldier of the 95th (Rifles) during the Peninsular Campaign of the Napoleonic Wars

**WITH WELLINGTON'S LIGHT CAVALRY** *by William Tomkinson*—The Experiences of an officer of the 16th Light Dragoons in the Peninsular and Waterloo campaigns of the Napoleonic Wars.

**SURTEES OF THE RIFLES** by *William Surtees*—A Soldier of the 95th (Rifles) in the Peninsular campaign of the Napoleonic Wars.

**ENSIGN BELL IN THE PENINSULAR WAR** *by George Bell*—The Experiences of a young British Soldier of the 34th Regiment 'The Cumberland Gentlemen' in the Napoleonic wars.

**WITH THE LIGHT DIVISION** by *John H. Cooke*—The Experiences of an Officer of the 43rd Light Infantry in the Peninsula and South of France During the Napoleonic Wars

**NAPOLEON'S IMPERIAL GUARD: FROM MARENGO TO WATERLOO** by *J. T. Headley*—This is the story of Napoleon's Imperial Guard from the bearskin caps of the grenadiers to the flamboyance of their mounted chasseurs, their principal characters and the men who commanded them.

**BATTLES & SIEGES OF THE PENINSULAR WAR** by *W. H. Fitchett*—Corunna, Busaco, Albuera, Ciudad Rodrigo, Badajos, Salamanca, San Sebastian & Others

# ALSO FROM LEONAUR

**AVAILABLE IN SOFTCOVER OR HARDCOVER WITH DUST JACKET**

**WELLINGTON AND THE PYRENEES CAMPAIGN VOLUME I: FROM VITORIA TO THE BIDASSOA** *by F. C. Beatson*—The final phase of the campaign in the Iberian Peninsula.

**WELLINGTON AND THE INVASION OF FRANCE VOLUME II: THE BIDASSOA TO THE BATTLE OF THE NIVELLE** *by F. C. Beatson*—The second of Beatson's series on the fall of Revolutionary France published by Leonaur, the reader is once again taken into the centre of Wellington's strategic and tactical genius.

**WELLINGTON AND THE FALL OF FRANCE VOLUME III: THE GAVES AND THE BATTLE OF ORTHEZ** by *F. C. Beatson*—This final chapter of F. C. Beatson's brilliant trilogy shows the 'captain of the age' at his most inspired and makes all three books essential additions to any Peninsular War library.

**NAVAL BATTLES OF THE NAPOLEONIC WARS** *by W. H. Fitchett*—Cape St. Vincent, the Nile, Cadiz, Copenhagen, Trafalgar & Others

**SERGEANT GUILLEMARD: THE MAN WHO SHOT NELSON?** *by Robert Guillemard*—A Soldier of the Infantry of the French Army of Napoleon on Campaign Throughout Europe

**WITH THE GUARDS ACROSS THE PYRENEES** by *Robert Batty*—The Experiences of a British Officer of Wellington's Army During the Battles for the Fall of Napoleonic France, 1813.

**A STAFF OFFICER IN THE PENINSULA** *by E. W. Buckham*—An Officer of the British Staff Corps Cavalry During the Peninsula Campaign of the Napoleonic Wars

**THE LEIPZIG CAMPAIGN: 1813—NAPOLEON AND THE "BATTLE OF THE NATIONS"** *by F. N. Maude*—Colonel Maude's analysis of Napoleon's campaign of 1813.

**BUGEAUD: A PACK WITH A BATON** by *Thomas Robert Bugeaud*—The Early Campaigns of a Soldier of Napoleon's Army Who Would Become a Marshal of France.

## TWO LEONAUR ORIGINALS

**SERGEANT NICOL** by *Daniel Nicol*—The Experiences of a Gordon Highlander During the Napoleonic Wars in Egypt, the Peninsula and France.

**WATERLOO RECOLLECTIONS** by *Frederick Llewellyn*—Rare First Hand Accounts, Letters, Reports and Retellings from the Campaign of 1815.

# ALSO FROM LEONAUR

## AVAILABLE IN SOFTCOVER OR HARDCOVER WITH DUST JACKET

**THE JENA CAMPAIGN: 1806** *by F. N. Maude*—The Twin Battles of Jena & Auerstadt Between Napoleon's French and the Prussian Army.

**PRIVATE O'NEIL** *by Charles O'Neil*—The recollections of an Irish Rogue of H. M. 28th Regt.—The Slashers— during the Peninsula & Waterloo campaigns of the Napoleonic wars.

**ROYAL HIGHLANDER** by *James Anton*—A soldier of H.M 42nd (Royal) Highlanders during the Peninsular, South of France & Waterloo Campaigns of the Napoleonic Wars.

**CAPTAIN BLAZE** *by Elzéar Blaze*—Elzéar Blaze recounts his life and experiences in Napoleon's army in a well written, articulate and companionable style.

**LEJEUNE VOLUME 1** by *Louis-François Lejeune*—The Napoleonic Wars through the Experiences of an Officer on Berthier's Staff.

**LEJEUNE VOLUME 2** by *Louis-François Lejeune*—The Napoleonic Wars through the Experiences of an Officer on Berthier's Staff.

**FUSILIER COOPER** *by John S. Cooper*—Experiences in the 7th (Royal) Fusiliers During the Peninsular Campaign of the Napoleonic Wars and the American Campaign to New Orleans.

**CAPTAIN COIGNET** *by Jean-Roch Coignet*—A Soldier of Napoleon's Imperial Guard from the Italian Campaign to Russia and Waterloo.

**FIGHTING NAPOLEON'S EMPIRE** by *Joseph Anderson*—The Campaigns of a British Infantryman in Italy, Egypt, the Peninsular & the West Indies During the Napoleonic Wars.

**CHASSEUR BARRES** by *Jean-Baptiste Barres*—The experiences of a French Infantryman of the Imperial Guard at Austerlitz, Jena, Eylau, Friedland, in the Peninsular, Lutzen, Bautzen, Zinnwald and Hanau during the Napoleonic Wars.

**MARINES TO 95TH (RIFLES)** by *Thomas Fernyhough*—The military experiences of Robert Fernyhough during the Napoleonic Wars.

**HUSSAR ROCCA** by *Albert Jean Michel de Rocca*—A French cavalry officer's experiences of the Napoleonic Wars and his views on the Peninsular Campaigns against the Spanish, British And Guerilla Armies.

**SERGEANT BOURGOGNE** by *Adrien Bourgogne*—With Napoleon's Imperial Guard in the Russian Campaign and on the Retreat from Moscow 1812 - 13.

# ALSO FROM LEONAUR

www.ingramcontent.com/pod-product-compliance
Lightning Source LLC
LaVergne TN
LVHW090950080826
845145LV00003B/961

* 9 7 8 1 8 4 6 7 7 5 3 7 6 *